MIDNIGHT WATER

GAYLENE PERRY

MIDNIGHT WATER

A MEMOIR

PICADOR
Pan Macmillan Australia

The names of most of the people appearing in this book have been changed to preserve their privacy. Likewise, the name of the town of Ironbark is fictionalised.

First published 2004 in Picador by Pan Macmillan Australia Pty Limited
St Martins Tower, 31 Market Street, Sydney

Copyright © Gaylene Perry 2004

All rights reserved. No part of this book may be reproduced or transmitted in any form or by any means, electronic, mechanical, including photocopying, recording or by any information storage and retrieval system, without prior permission in writing from the publisher.

National Library of Australia
Cataloguing-in-Publication data:

Perry, Gaylene.
Midnight water : a memoir.

ISBN 0 330 36467 7.

1. Perry, Gaylene. 2. Bereavement. 3. Sudden death.
I. Title

155.937092

Papers used by Pan Macmillan Australia Pty Ltd are natural, recyclable products made from wood grown in sustainable forests. The manufacturing processes conform to the environmental regulations of the country of origin.

Set in 10.5/18 pt New Caledonia by Midland Typesetters
Printed in Australia by McPherson's Printing Group

To my father
To my brother
And to all those who filled my grandparents'
house with love and strength in the week
following 2 January 1993

Where have you gone? The tide is over you,
The turn of midnight water's over you,
As Time is over you, and mystery,
And memory, the flood that does not flow.

Kenneth Slessor

1

Saturday, 2 January 1993, 6 pm

They loll on their unmade bed, grains of beach sand sifting through the layers of tussled sheets. Gaylene is twenty-three and her boyfriend, Jude, is twenty-seven.

Twenty-seven is the age that her mother, Glenda, pretended to be for five years after her actual twenty-seventh birthday, not wanting to be thirty, to be old. On the day she turned twenty-seven her husband, William, bought her – or as she is wont to say, bought himself – a stereo record player. They had no money. Both of them worked at the meatworks down the highway, Glenda weighing sheep and hosing killing floors on nightshift, William butchering on dayshift.

They had recently had to hide their bottle-green bomb of a car at someone else's place to stop it from being repossessed. When Glenda saw the record player she stormed from the house, that flat-roofed fibro-cement house in Donald, got into the bottle-green bomb and backed down the driveway. William went after her and she ran over one of his feet. She said later that it was an accident. While he was hopping she took off in the opposite direction to the meatworks, down the dirt service road that ran beside the highway.

Twenty-seven is one of those numbers that sticks in Gaylene's mind even now as she lies spread out on her stomach on the bed in the house that she and Jude share in Maud Street, North Balwyn. The number 1978 also sticks in her mind since that was the year her father went to Papua New Guinea, when he volunteered to help build a dam in a village in the highlands that visitors could reach only in a light plane that had to land on a thin airstrip hewn into the side of a jungle-tangled mountain. William was gone for a month but to her at the age of nine it felt like half of her life passed while he was away, like years passed between each letter he sent, every story he sent: pale-blue tissue paper stories in envelopes with birds of paradise on the stamps. She learned the name like one long lyrical birdcall of a word. *Birdsofparadise*. Her father was with birdsofparadise in Papua New Guinea.

Glenda arranged for a family portrait to be taken before William left. She joked for years that she had been scared he would not come back from Papua New Guinea, that he would meet with an accident there. But he did come back, tanned, muscled, bearded, and then two weeks after his return the light plane pilot who had flown him in and landed him on the jungle airstrip died when his plane crashed into the mountainside.

By the time William and Glenda came to be living in Donald (the year that Gaylene started school), they had already lived together in houses in Ironbark, Inglewood and Charlton, as William moved from butchery to butchery to meatworks after it was decided that he could no longer work for his father, Leonard, whom everyone called Leo except for his grandchildren, who called him Papa. Every Friday

William quit or Leo sacked him. It was time to move on. And on and on. They followed the roads between one dusty hot town in north-central Victoria and another. Together they had four children: Brad and Gaylene and the twins, Scott and Katy. The twins were still babies and had to be dropped off at a babysitter's before six every morning between the change of shifts at the meatworks.

In Gaylene and Jude's bed the sand spreads like coarse brown sugar every time one of them flings out a limb to try to find a cool spot on the sheets. A fan oscillates on its tall stalk, shifting hot air. The beach at Point Ormond in Elwood had been too hot this afternoon; they had run into a friend, his windsurfer sail lying limp and dimpled on the grass by the esplanade. The water was flat and thick-looking. The friend slid the batons out of his sail and they waved to him and turned back to drive home, towels thrown over the baking cracked brown vinyl seats of their car.

Point Ormond is already part of the story of Gaylene's relationship with Jude. When they first met three years earlier, they parked there and ate hotdogs

Jude bought from a 7-Eleven. It was the year before she stopped eating meat and she was broke. Most of her family had taken off to live in Darwin, and she was sharing a flat with people who were as broke as herself. Today, through the heat, Point Ormond behind them, Gaylene and Jude headed for the clinker brick house in Maud Street that they have been renting for a couple of years. They picked up a cold bottle of soft drink and the fat layers of the Saturday *Age*, and then, still in their bathing suits, crossed the lawn, the grass crinkly and dry under their bare feet. The neighbours who grow sunflowers like a tall fence of faces around their own clinker brick house ('Sunflowers are everywhere in Greece, dear') were nowhere to be seen. Maud Street was empty but for the noise of air-conditioners and the almost audible heat haze coming off the paths. Inside the couple closed all the blinds, flipped on the fan, and threw themselves down in the mussed-up bed that they had only climbed out of a few hours ago.

Now she picks up the glossy weekend magazine from the newspaper, frowning when she sees that it is thinner than usual: even the newspaper people are still on holidays.

Muffled by the fan's noisy vibrating, the phone rings, a sluggish mile away in the dining room.

'You get it.'

'No, you.'

Giggling, teasing, canoodling, it goes on and the ringing goes on with it, then stops, then starts again, and she gives in, tossing down the magazine, seeing it take up a furious flickering powered by the fan.

'Your turn next time.' She runs to catch the phone before the answering machine cuts in.

'Hello, love.' A pause. 'Is Jude there with you?'

That sounds like her grandfather's voice: Leo's voice, Papa's voice. But he has never called her before except on her birthday and he has never asked directly for Jude, and his tone is not like one she has ever heard from him. When she speaks she finds that a polite little girl's voice takes over her own: she says she will get Jude and she rests the receiver on top of a pine chest of drawers and goes back to the bedroom.

In the time it takes her to walk there her feet start to feel heavy and the air around her seems charged.

'It's Papa. He wants to talk to you. Something is wrong. I know it.'

Jude struggles to get up, hurries to the phone.

The fan still blows like a fool. It moves her hair as she passes in front of it, and the glossy magazine pages flap away like wide tongues poking at her.

She can hear Jude in the dining room. 'No, no, no.' He starts to weep, the kind of weeping rarely heard in everyday life: deep, hoarse, primal.

She rushes to the bedroom door and pushes it shut, but that is not enough to block the noise and it builds up like pressure in her ears. A desire comes over her, a desire she wants to shake off. It scares her like she imagines that suddenly having the urge to take off her clothes in public might make her feel. She rushes over to stand by the corner window, by her desk, the desk that her father found for her at the Camberwell Market, the desk with the water-warped top. She wants to get under the desk.

Whatever is being said on the phone has not caught up with her yet but it towers over her in a wave; its motion has started and she knows it will not be stopped. And all she can do is look for a place to hide. This desire returns to her like a refrain from early childhood, as though life is only a moment's passing and it is not twenty years but two seconds ago that she was three and wearing a white organdy dress with pink velvet flocking. She was to be immunised that day, she was to have a needle at the kindergarten, and when the time came to leave for the kindergarten she looked for a place to hide. She hid under her brother Brad's bed, finding a lost Little Golden Book under there and looking at the pictures of glowing-haired, glowing-winged angels on the pages while Glenda and Brad called her and she did not answer; she was hiding.

Brad found her. He is twenty months older than Gaylene, they had grown from babyhood together. His face appeared at the side of the bed and she watched him consider what to do, to dob or not to dob, and she looked into his face and silently pleaded, and he kept his eyes on her while he called to Glenda and said he had found Gaylene. He shrugged at her as though to say that she knew she must have her needle. And now, again, she needs a place to hide but she will be found, she must be found.

Someone is dead. She can guess that much. And it must be someone close to her. In the past she has lost nobody closer than one distant grandparent. One day in a house in the Mallee, in Wycheproof, where they lived after Donald, after the meatworks, she sat on a lime-green vinyl chair at a round laminex table with her family, eating fish and chips, William telling a black joke, the rest of them laughing, drinking Coke, dumping pools of tomato sauce onto the corners of the fish and chip paper, and she told herself that her family was charmed, that nobody in her family would die until they were old, as old as her great-grandparents. She could not imagine it being otherwise and if she could not imagine it then it must not be real, would never be real.

Now the possibilities race through her. Jude's cries grow louder.

Is her whole family dead? Why is it that Leo has made the call? Why has anyone made the call, why is nobody here at the door, at the house?

She is shrivelling, turning selfish, she can think only of herself, of what is being brought into her house, her room, her body, her self. She senses her wounds like a battered accident victim who is talking and perhaps even walking and is the only one who does not know that she is already dead, already gone. Inside she is bleeding, gushing with blood, family blood, but she still cannot tell which part of her is slashed or severed. Or can she?

It is Dad. William. She does not know how but she knows it. William is dead.

And then she remembers, the past flowing through her in a rapid current: following the fish and chips, following the thought about being charmed, a time came when she did indeed imagine one of her family dead. She had imagined William dead. She was fourteen, still living in the Mallee, and her parents were running their own butchery.

This was the first of the butcheries that William

and Glenda owned and in 1979 they had built it up new from the remains of an opportunity shop. Tired of the meatworks in Donald, the family had driven around looking at butcheries for sale. Gaylene's favourite was in South Gippsland. She was almost ten and she had chosen that butchery because it was in a town with dark green hills and a faint smell of the ocean. But the butchery was too expensive, as were all of the butcheries that the family looked at. Instead they moved to the Mallee, to Wycheproof, a town sliced through by the Calder Highway and the railway line that ran straight along the middle of the main street, a town quilted all around with flat pale paddocks of wheat and sealed under a hot solid blue dome of sky. This landscape was the one that Gaylene and her brother Brad would know throughout most of the years of their adolescence. William and Glenda leased the old shop that had been an opportunity shop and set about making it into a butchery. William lined the shop section with dark brown timber panelling and put in benchtops of bright blue. Sawdust was spread over the concrete floor. A new coolroom with white laminated walls was installed behind the shop section and new sinks were put out the back where the mincer would go, where the washing tubs sat on the floor, ready to be filled with hot soapy water.

The butchery was down the street from the weatherboard house where they lived, the house on the main road, opposite the old steam train set in concrete, the real train tracks running almost past their front door. One night, ten o'clock, winter, a thick pure-white Mallee frost rested on every surface outside, yet Gaylene left her bedroom to go jump on the trampoline. Through the lounge room, walking behind the heads of her family watching television from the couch, she went outside, needing to think, needing to jump out the energy that was fizzing inside her. This happened often at that time. As she sat in her room dressed for bed, finishing homework or reading books or writing in one of her diaries, energy built up in her until she felt restless, and then she would pull a jumper over the top of her nightie and go to the trampoline out by the bare branches of the apricot tree. While she jumped on the trampoline she thought. She told herself stories that were like dreams but felt real. And that night as she jumped she thought her father dead.

He lay in a shallow open grave at the back of a cemetery with yellow stony dirt on the ground. The grave was too short for him, he lay in it as though it were a bathtub, with his head and shoulders poking out at one end and his calves and feet out at the other end. He was crying like a child. She wanted to comfort him but she knew that she could not make him undead. She gave him a teddy bear and he held it to his chest, saying: 'It's not time yet. It's not time.' On the trampoline she jumped higher, shattering the ice, the frost, into long flat shards, and the longer she jumped the more the shards shattered and dissolved into a cold slush of powder that bounced up around her knees. After a while the powder melted to a cold slick that shone in the moonlight and she was sweating. She pulled off her jumper and lay on the cool mat of the trampoline in her short sleeveless nightie. By then she was sobbing. As she lay on the wet vinyl mat the front door to the house creaked open and then clicked firmly shut, but she took little notice and soon she was cold and clammy and she climbed down from the trampoline and went inside.

William, with fear in his face, shouted at her, wanting to know where she had been, would not believe that she was on the trampoline this late on a cold night and, besides, he looked and she was not there. She let him shout. She could not tell him that she was lying there crying, imagining that he was dead and that she was overcome with grief at the thought.

'I can't, I just can't,' she hears Jude saying now, but she wills him to come to her. She needs to be told what has happened. She is ready, impatient, to hear it.

The phone is put down with a clunking sound on the drawers and he comes to her, his footsteps soft on the carpet; he opens the bedroom door and here he is and she moves away from the desk, the corner window, and the urge to hide. From his face she sees that now he is hiding. He cannot bring himself to tell her, to be the one to tell her.

'Who is it?'

'It's your Dad –'

The words almost bounce off her: she can nearly make it not hurt. In this instant the truth is hardly different to what she imagined on the trampoline, the death on the trampoline, the bathtub grave. It does hurt, yet from a long way away, not quite touching her.

But Jude has not finished his sentence.

There beside the door, beside the unmade bed in the messy room, her boyfriend's lips are still moving. His voice that she always thinks of as her sanctuary is broken up but he is still speaking.

'And Brad. Your father, and Brad, both died.'

This penetrates.

Brad. Her closest brother, closest sibling in age and affection, the brother she feels webbed to, the brother she and Jude lived with in a house in Brunswick a couple of years ago, her gentle, quiet brother.

'How?'

The details are vague, the words do not fit together: a waterfall, one man falling over a waterfall, one trying to save the other; the words are discordant, wrong, jammed together. She asks which waterfall, where? Jude does not know. She thinks, tries to place her family, to locate exactly where they should be today, and she remembers that William and Glenda are in Ironbark, staying in a hired caravan at Bushy's, the family land, Glenda's ancestors' land, where William has been laying the foundations of a house he is going to build, a mudbrick house that she thinks of as their first real family home even though she is unlikely to ever live in this house. William and Glenda are due back in Melbourne this weekend, today, now, for tomorrow night all of the family is expected at the weekly Sunday night dinner: roast dinner around the table in the house in Elm Street, Northcote, that William and Glenda and the twins have lived in since they landed back in the state after a period of living in Darwin. And Brad should be at home, he lives in Fitzroy now, he works in a video shop in St Kilda; it is Saturday night, he must be rostered on.

Bushy's. The town of Ironbark. Central Victoria.

Box ironbark trees. Wattle. Bush orchids. Yellow stony dirt. Gold. Quartz. Mineshafts. No waterfalls.

Waterfall. It is the sort of word she likes, she cannot help that: even now in her head she sees images of moist dark green foliage, ferns, and clear white cascading water. She has visions of a set of falls near Bendigo, where on another hot day years ago she swam naked in the cold calm water below the falls, cupping handfuls of the water to drink. She chases away the thoughts, the images, almost before they come: stupid thoughts, crazy images, but not as crazy as the other images, the visions of Dad and Brad brought together today, displaced, dislocated, and then tumbling over a precipice, past a frill of ferns, falling over falls.

They both died.

Her father is forty-five and her brother is twenty-five. And both men are dead.

She is smaller now, smaller than the girl who wanted to hide; she is shrinking, she cannot speak above a whisper. Her legs do not work. She fumbles back to find the edge of the bed, the fan's breeze scares her, anything moving scares her, time passing scares her.

Her family is still on the telephone, Jude says. Not her grandfather now but her cousin Marcus. He is also in the country, yet he should be at home in the city, in his old art deco flat in St Kilda, working at the video shop, the same one where Brad works: Brad, his cousin, his lifelong best friend. Marcus wants to talk to her, Jude says, but she will not talk, she does not want to talk to anyone. He goes back to the dining room and this time the doors between the rooms are open and all the sounds are clear and sharp, for the wave of apprehension has crashed and spent itself.

'She's gone all quiet,' he tells Marcus. 'She didn't say anything, really.' Yes, shock, he says, and she sees him nodding. She gets up from the bed.

One step in front of another, bare feet on carpet, sand on carpet, she walks past him. He hesitates, must think she has changed her mind about the phone, but she keeps walking, past the dining table that William made for them, put in their house after they moved out of Brunswick and came here to live in their own place. They had no furniture, not until William started building pieces for them and picking up other pieces from the markets that he loved to trawl. She has not changed her mind about the phone; she has left the bedroom for only one reason. Water. Her throat is dry, choked. The rest of the house is oven-like, the musty venetian blinds shut to keep out the heat, the doors and windows closed. From the kitchen dresser, the grubby dresser painted with house paint, the dresser that bothers her now, dirty, messy, for she feels on display, raw, exposed, she takes a glass and watches herself carry it – without trembling, almost normally, one hand wrapped around the glass – to the sink. She fills it from the cold water tap, drinks it in slow gulps, then fills it again, drinks again. Her throat is still parched and the water does not seem to touch it.

Later it will sicken her to think of how she filled herself with water, drank the water, let it slip over her tongue.

He has hung up. They are to go to Ironbark, he tells her, they are to find Scott and then they are to go to Ironbark. He is to bring her mother's kids to her; she wants them with her.

Gaylene sees that he is weeping again, he has spoken to Glenda, heard her voice. To Gaylene he seems a long way away and she feels herself prickling up, wanting to say no, that she will stay here, she does not want to leave the house. He sobs. She can almost see herself reaching out to wipe the tears with her fingertips, the soft hands that he loves. Almost. But she cannot seem to make the action happen.

'I have to tell Scott,' he says. 'Scott doesn't know yet. They didn't want either of you to be told by the police.'

No, she thinks. She herself must tell her little brother. She says this to Jude and relief floods his face.

She peels off her pink and black bathing suit and picks up a summer skirt and t-shirt from the bathroom floor and puts them on. She looks for clothes to fill her backpack, her uni backpack, but everything is dirty, the closets are empty as usual, the laundry overdue to be done. She throws in a handful of half-clean garments and as they are about to leave Jude breaks down and kneels on the floor.

Again she wants to comfort him, she imagines she sees her arms going around him; she does put one hand onto one of his shoulders but it feels like nothing, like it is weightless.

He gets up and follows her, keeping close, as she presses the stop button of the oscillating fan and the glossy magazine finally lies still on the bedsheets.

2

Saturday, 2 January 1993, 7 pm

They cross the city. She sees none of it, does not know if the drive is fast and smooth or traffic-clogged and laboured. Nothing is visible to her but a glassy haze through the car windows. This drive feels like being on an aeroplane, she thinks: she is suspended, encased, yet the undertow of a sense of danger is never far away.

Jude keeps reaching out a hand to place on her right thigh, he keeps looking at her, checking on her, silently begging her to speak, to respond to him, but all that she will let herself think about is how thirsty she is and how badly she needs to pee and finally what words she will find to say to Scott. What if he is not at home? She knows little of his life and could never find him if he were at a friend's house or out partying. Mentally she tries to pin him down at home. Or maybe if he is out she will find him nearby, walking down the street, coming out of the milk bar on St Georges Road or having a smoke in the Batman Gardens.

And then she remembers, how could she have forgotten, how could she have not thought? Katy.

'Where's Katy? Who'll tell her?' She pictures her sister, slim and fragile. Already Gaylene senses the sadness that will be in Katy's eyes, the family midbrown eyes, the same as Gaylene's: golden ochre, Jude calls the colour.

'Katy knows. She's there.'

Gaylene's sense of dislocation worsens. Katy should not be in Ironbark today. Jude puts his hand back on Gaylene's thigh and leaves it there as they turn into Elm Street, Northcote, and pull up near the gates of the house and get out.

The curtains on the bay window in the lounge room are open. The window is open, she can see the fabric lifting in a breeze that has picked up. The smell of rain is in the air and an hour or two must have passed already since the sound of the phone ringing broke into the afternoon. Storm clouds have flooded the summer blue from the sky, turning the evening dark too early. The television screen shows through the window, too bright, for now the sky is growing thick and heavy and the greenish light of the approaching storm is all around and the television screen glows through this light and hurts her eyes. The television, the open window: she knows that Scott is home. She must go in. If the curtain wavers a bit more or if he gets up to change the channel or if the ad break comes on and he gets up to make a coffee or go to the toilet he may see her standing here at the open ironwork gates, feeling the concrete still hot from the day through the soles of her sandals.

Jude is two steps ahead of her, looking back, wanting to look after her, to take it slowly for her. He is also anxious to go inside to do the job that her family has asked him to do. But he hesitates, not just, she knows, to wait for her to move inside the gates. They both know that the moment will come soon enough.

They will have to tell Scott. Here at the gates with light raindrops falling on her arms she wants to stay and let him watch his television show a little longer, maybe see how pretty the night is turning after the stinking day and think of his parents on the block at Ironbark and wonder how much work Dad got done on the house during his holiday. The block of land is partly owned by Scott. He and Brad inherited it from Bushy, the great-uncle who had been the last to live there. Scott and Brad are letting their parents build the family home on the land. She wants to stand at the gates and be rained on and let Scott live a few more minutes of his eighteen-year-old life before he is scarred by the words she must tell him.

A sound comes through the window, maybe a shuffling of feet in shoes on the polished wooden coffee table that Scott would not put his feet on if his mother were home. Jude walks up the path, his head turned toward her.

'I don't know how,' she says.

'There's no right way to tell him,' he answers, and already he sounds knowing and experienced. For the first time since the phone call she feels his closeness, hears the sanctuary in him, and she unplants her feet and follows him up to the edge of the concrete porch and then she moves in front of him and knocks softly, too softly. He reaches around her and knocks again, louder.

The feet clamber down from the tabletop. Gaylene and Jude hear Scott stomp along the creaking carpeted floorboards, clearing his throat – like a man, she thinks; her little brother sounds like a man. The front light comes on with the throw of a heavy old switch. The door opens and one of her hands flies up to catch hold of Jude.

Scott smiles when he sees them. 'Come early for Sunday dinner?'

Scott. He is taller than her now and his smile is warm, sure of her, sure of her and Jude. The smile is a long way from the years when they were childhood rivals – more than that: they were enemies. She knows that as a little girl she was bossy toward the twins, Scott and Katy, and then as a teenager she was depressed, trapped in a bush town that she hated, and he was dark-tempered, volatile, even though he could be mellow, wrapping himself around Glenda for hugs, offering his mouth for kisses, chanting I-love-you. Scott and Gaylene clashed seemingly from the day the twins arrived when she was five and unhappy about being hoisted from the position of baby of the family by not one infant but two.

When she was sixteen, shortly after they had all escaped from Wycheproof, she made him angry one day and he picked up a heavy-based chair, one of the familiar lime-green vinyl swivel chairs left over from the seventies, and threw it at her and the heavy metal base of it caught her right cheekbone, gave her a black eye to show off when she went to her new school the next day. But now she prefers to think of him when he was fifteen, for that was the beginning of better times, of a slowly burgeoning friendship between them, the beginning of this smile on the concrete porch.

Scott had been in Darwin with their parents and Katy, and he was to return a couple of weeks before his mother and Katy made their way back. He did not want to travel home across the desert in a small car with Glenda and Katy. Gaylene was not clear about why the three of them were coming back to Victoria: the word was that Glenda hated Darwin and wanted to come home with or without William. Home. What that meant, her eldest daughter did not know: the family had no home as far as she could see at the time. Nevertheless they were coming. Scott had taken a coach and train trip, had been travelling for days across to Cairns and then down the east coast, and the next day he would come into Spencer Street Station. Glenda phoned the Brunswick house, phoning for Brad, but Gaylene and Jude were sharing the house with Brad and his girlfriend, Nicola, and Gaylene picked up the phone. Glenda told Gaylene the time that Scott needed to be picked up. Gaylene knew that Brad would be working at that time. He had a job as a waiter in an Italian restaurant, dressing up in a white shirt and black pants every lunchtime and driving his car into Carlton for his shifts, then coming home afterwards to sit and draw by the large window at the back of the house, to work on his illustrations, his black bitser dog at his feet, his two tabby cats up on the desk, sunning beside the glass. He would be at work when Scott's train came in but she and Jude had the day off and she told Glenda that they would drive in to pick up Scott.

Glenda sounded uncertain. Maybe she did not trust her daughter: Gaylene knew she had not been what Glenda would call *big on family* for a few years and of course Gaylene and Scott had never been friendly, and Glenda did not know Jude, did not know how he fitted in, as she would say. Gaylene told her mother that Scott would be picked up. She wished she could tell her that she was different now: she was away from the boyfriend that she'd had before the family left for Darwin, the boyfriend her parents hated, the boyfriend with the Torana car, and she had spent time with Brad and she had Jude for a friend. If only, she thought as she hung up the phone, she could have brought herself to tell her mother, way back before Glenda had left for Darwin, what the boyfriend had been doing to her daughter. Glenda had an inkling though: Gaylene believed that. One day before

Darwin Glenda said to her, 'I had a terrible dream about you last night. You were standing in front of me and you were crying. You were saying, "Help, Mum, I'm hurt. I'm hurt." And I woke up and lay there thinking I should call you, then told myself not to be ridiculous. Still, I could not get back to sleep for hours.' Gaylene said nothing. She looked away and soon she left the house with the boyfriend, got into the Torana, and let him drive her away. She was shaking, for at the same time Glenda had had that dream, the boyfriend had Gaylene lying on the concrete of a car park, him sitting astride her, his knees pinning down her elbows, slapping her face one cheek at a time.

She wanted to be the one to pick up Scott from Spencer Street; she wanted to see him, to let him, for a start, know that she had changed.

She and Jude stood on the lino by the cafés at the station and Scott walked down the ramp from a platform. He had shot up, grown up, his voice cracking, limbs showing hints of the great height he would soon reach. His skin was deeply tanned and he had grown his hair long; like her own it was dark chocolate in colour. She moved toward him, smiling. They did not hug or kiss, had never hugged or kissed. He hardly smiled: the old enmity was in his face along with the sulkiness of a teenager who has been in transit for too many days. But in the car he opened a green army rucksack, their father's rucksack, and pulled out a dog-eared soggy-looking book for her to see. He passed the book to her through the gap between the front seats. It was *The Hobbit*.

'You read it, then?' she asked. He said he loved it and he had not been able to stop reading it all the way down from the north. The book had been from her. It was a gift, a birthday present she sent a few weeks earlier with Brad, who had flown up to Darwin to visit the family and then came home saying: 'Mum's had it. She and the twins are coming back. Could've told me before I bought the plane ticket.'

She had sent Scott this book as Glenda said he had started reading books, fantasy books, and Gaylene thought of *The Hobbit*. The book had once been read to her in a classroom in Wycheproof. She turned *The Hobbit* in her hands. It felt hot, damp, and she thought she sensed a steaminess in it; this book in heat-buckled covers seemed to hold the feel of where it had been.

Light shines out of the passage at the Elm Street house and behind Scott she sees the ornamental table with teetering legs that William found for Glenda at a secondhand shop, and on the table is the kerosene lamp with the oyster glass shade, a lamp from the old pioneer house at Bushy's. Glenda bought that lamp at the auction that was held after Gaylene's great-uncle, Bushy, had died.

Scott asks what is wrong, looking from Gaylene to Jude. Later he will say that it was the expression in their eyes that warned him, that made the possibilities start to burst forth in his head, made him wonder if she was all he had left: one sister standing there in the dishwater dark of Elm Street.

They all move inside. Jude presses them into the passage, into the lounge room with its family furniture: the couch with the exposed timber arms and legs and the brown tweed upholstery; the matching coffee table; the matching armchair with the bottom falling out – the one that William was going to mend years ago. The commercials are loud on the television but Jude switches it off. And she thinks of the television wars between Scott and their father, the arguments over which channel they would watch, the surly way Scott had of entering a room and changing the channel when William was already watching a program and how this made William furious.

Awkwardly Scott stands by the broken chair and she and Jude come to stand in front of him, their backs to the window. It feels like they are looming, do not fit into the room. She tries to speak, her mouth as dry as bones.

Jude hugs her tightly from behind. She says, 'Scott, we have to tell you something terrible.'

She remembers that back at Maud Street she had needed to know as quickly as possible who it was that had been affected by whatever had happened. For Scott she tries to get at least that out.

'It's Dad and Brad. Dad and Brad have both been killed.'

Out of her mouth a news headline has jumped. A headline word. Killed. Like in a road accident. Killed.

Scott falls back into the chair, sinking into the broken base. His large long hands are held out, rigid, on the timber chair arms: they look just like his father's hands.

She and Jude try to tell him what has happened but they stumble, they do not have enough information. Waterfall. Falling over. One after the other.

Gaylene speaks, trying to make sense. The pieces do have a kind of sense as a story if she puts them together in a certain way, although it is not a story that matches her family and its landscapes, its locations. But it is a narrative, it is a structure, and the three of them let themselves hold on to it for now like holding on to a sturdy handle to steady themselves. It even helps, she thinks, to know that the waterfall story does not ring with truth. If it were to sound like truth, then Dad and Brad must indeed be dead. Killed. And yet Dad and Brad are here, in the house, in her, in Scott, even in Jude. They are in Brad's framed cartoons propped on the dining table: a present to his mother on Christmas Day just a week ago. And William: his clothes are in his wardrobe. If she looks his Driza-bone will be there, the greasy coat he paid a couple of dollars for at a trash and treasure market. His nail clippers will be in the bathroom, or perhaps in a junk drawer in the kitchen: he has gnarled toenails on his long hammer-toed feet and it is typical of his humour to seek out the clippers and clip the yellow whorls of nail out in the lounge room, waiting to be told off, loving it. She can hear his laugh: he cannot be dead. Yes, the three of them here grasp on to the waterfall story, needing sense but not too much sense.

'Mum's waiting for us.'

'Give me a minute. I need to call a mate.' He leaves the room, pulls a phone into his bedroom, closes the door, the phone cord a tense snake along the floor.

Thirsty, so thirsty. She goes towards the kitchen through the dining room and there she pauses, feet heavy, body weighed down. The wall of photographs stops her. She can see only the top half of the wall, for under the photographs there is a dining table. The table has a straight grain almost like ruled lines and its surface is satin-smooth and the colour of redgum honey in a glass jar.

The table dates from the time in the late eighties when the family had sold the Wycheproof butchery and moved to Bendigo, creating another butchery from scratch. It was the prettiest of the butcheries, painted in heritage colours and housed in an historic building in the city. For a moment it seemed the business would be prosperous but bills started going unpaid, and one night William had a heart attack at a pub. He later told Gaylene that he felt like he had been plunged underwater and could not breathe or speak. The word *receivership* started being whispered around the house and soon the newest butchery passed out of William and Glenda's hands. It was during the short moment when the business had looked set to prosper that the honeyed table entered the house in Bendigo that the family had moved into.

The Bendigo home was modern brick, the kind of home that Glenda had spoken of wanting in the past. And it was in the same street as her best friend's house, a street of well-watered green lawns and beds of petunias, with a park and playground at one end.

This house became filled with furniture that she and William chose together: a colonial kitchen setting for meals with the kids, the timber and tweed suite in the lounge room, and this polished table with its matching leather upholstered chairs in the dining room. It had been the first time they could afford to choose furniture that they liked. Soon afterwards came the night in the pub when William found himself unable to speak. He knew it was his heart but he could not find the voice to tell anyone. He was thirty-seven and a slim strong man. Nobody on the pub stools around him suspected a heart attack.

Now the honeyed dining table stands in this house in Elm Street. Every Sunday night around the dining table that Glenda has kept polished over the years, the family sits for roast dinner and Gaylene sits for her vegetarian dinner as she has become a vegetarian despite being the daughter of parents who met on the road to a slaughterhouse. The Sunday dinners started after Darwin when the whole family came to live in the same city. None of them likes to miss the Sunday dinner around the table under the photographs.

Of those who come for dinner only William has his picture on the wall. The photographs, so goes the Sunday dinner joke, are of what the family call the dead people, and William's children find it funny that he has placed his own picture in the middle of them.

Among them are portraits of Glenda's great-great-grandparents, the pioneers who built the old house on Bushy's, the people who first owned the family land. The pioneers, Sarah and Dugald, migrated separately in the eighteen fifties. They built the house of timber and mud that still stands on the land and was last permanently occupied in the late nineteen seventies.

And there are pictures of William's grandparents, photographs he has recently restored and hand-tinted. She thinks he has the blue eyes of his grandmother exactly right. This woman is long dead, dead when her children were indeed still children. But she looks just like her eldest daughter, William's mother, and William's mother's eyes are Wedgwood blue: pale, opaque. William has tinted the eyes of the woman in the photographs a perfect shade of Wedgwood blue.

The picture of William in the middle of the wall display is sepia-toned. He is bearded; he has a dark bushy beard like the one to be seen in most photographs of Ned Kelly. The tip of the beard touches the top of his chest. He wears a white shirt with a pressed collar, buttons open at the neck. He looks directly out, unsmiling, his eyes soft and fluid and searching. It is an old-fashioned look that she thinks belongs here on the wall with the pictures from other decades and other centuries. Brad took the photograph of William. It was for a university assignment, part of his studies in graphic design. William had framed the print in one of the wooden frames he had started collecting along with other fragments of old homes and past lives.

She makes herself walk away from her father's gaze, his very-much alive gaze, and into the kitchen. Murky preserves in fat jars are lined up on top of the cupboards above the sink: his preserves. She imagines the kitchen smelling of garlic and oil, Glenda shaking her head and leaving him to it as long as he cleans up his mess afterwards and never asks her to taste anything from the jars, and Gaylene laughing at the murkiness, telling him to add more garlic for she loves garlic.

She drinks water, goes to the toilet, empties her bladder, drinks more water, hears Scott's bedroom door opening, his footsteps. It is his turn now to throw clothes into a bag. A roll of corned beef – silverside, butchers call it, and they slice it open to show the glittering look of the meat – boils in a lidless saucepan on the stove. Perhaps Glenda called earlier today, telling Scott to take the silverside out of the fridge, out of the freezer, and have it boiling through the afternoon ready for their dinner when they arrive home tonight. 'Turn this off?' Gaylene mumbles as Scott comes into the kitchen and picks up and pockets his wallet. He stares at her. She looks away, turns off the gas flame and, not knowing why, picks up the saucepan lid from the bench and puts it on the saucepan, covers the meat, covers their dinner for them.

Once more she drinks a glass of water. 'I can't stop drinking,' she says, and the words run out of her, small talk, small seepage to keep her afloat.

Outside Scott throws his bag into the hatchback of Jude's car and gets into the back seat, gangly, legs too long. She moves her front passenger seat forward. Jude drives out of Elm Street towards Sydney Road and then along the freeway. Inside the car nobody speaks. Jude starts to weep again.

Lightning crosses the turbulent sky.

3

Saturday, 2 January 1993, 8 pm

Out of the city, on the freeway, the car windows still look like frosted glass to her, a glass haze of headlights and trees and water droplets and the larger glass curve of the sky that pulses with lightning and migrating clouds. Jude is trying his hardest to be quiet: she can see that, she watches him. With his tears and the rain, he must hardly be able to see out of the windscreen. He is sobbing and neither she nor Scott can help him; they are rigid.

She has not shed a tear. She thinks that Scott also has not shed a tear.

One hand on the steering wheel, Jude leans over to her; he seems to want to collapse, a paper canoe taking on water, to want to stop being the driver, the one with the job: the policeman, the marshal, the children-deliverer. He keeps the car moving towards Ironbark, the town where Gaylene and Brad were born. But she thinks that he is imagining what he would like to do: career off the road, stop, be held, instead of having this job.

He is her lover. He is her best friend. A few weeks ago she learned that her father knows she loves Jude and even though she laughed at the time, giggled at her father's verdict of the future, she knows that William is rarely wrong or at least rarely wrong in her view. A butcher who was pulled out of school at the age of thirteen: she thinks of him as the smartest person she has ever known.

Indeed she loves Jude. Yet his hand clutching her thigh again and the floppy appearance of him as he tries to keep himself upright and his car on the road seem too visceral, too distant from the inchoate story she is clutching on to with its waterfall imagery and displaced characters and unthinkable climax.

The car feels like a fragile beetle on the freeway.

She senses its every jerk, shudder, slide, and she is aware of feeling less safe than she has ever felt in her life. It is too soon to grieve. Grief. The word will not become familiar for some time yet. But inside she has lost her sense of personal safety and the lightweight car on the wide wet road makes her nervous, as does Jude's weeping, his filmed eyes, his half-turning toward her.

She takes his hand. She squeezes. The hand feels like a rubber hand from a joke shop. Brad had one of those joke hands once: severed, daubed with red-paint blood at the wrist.

'It's all right,' she whispers.

His face is wet, slick as the road. 'It's not all right,' he answers. She squeezes again and tells him he must drive carefully. For her he eases off the accelerator, reluctantly puts both hands on the wheel. Scott fidgets, his knees bumping the back of her seat. He wants speed, she thinks, he wants to be there, to get to the end of the road. She wills Jude to keep the car under control.

His crying is unstoppable. In the face of this, let

alone everything else, Gaylene feels enclosed and distant and miserable. Before the phone call that brought the news, she had thought they had a solid relationship. Three years together had seemed like a long time. In their minds they had been adults, living in a house together, sharing a bed. But tonight it seems like they hardly know one another, like they are gawky adolescents who can barely shape words in their mouths to comfort one another and to face the situation they are driving towards.

Gaylene speaks: she needs to empty her bladder again. Scott sighs, seethes, his hands, Dad's hands, tensing, stretching, in front of him. She sees them over her left shoulder as Jude stops the car and she gets out and climbs down the side of the road and finds bushes to squat under, rain in the branches, water on her face, spiders in the trees that look too large, too close, too menacing.

Calmness settles over her as they move toward the Shepparton–Seymour turnoff. Jude's tears continue to wet his face. Her own face is smooth and wooden as though she cannot remember that she once knew how to cry. He cries for her, she thinks, and she settles back into her seat and lets him.

Up ahead over the distant hills a storm cracks and rumbles and fumes for her. She smiles to herself and quickly hides her mouth behind one hand even though the smile is for her father, for William, for his love of thunderstorms, the way thunderstorms seem to clear his blood, clear his mind. In the motion of the storm she thinks she can hear the *1812 Overture*, his favourite music, his thunderstorm music, and she is back in Donald, back in the days and nights of the meatworks, when he would play the *1812 Overture* on the record player, turning the fat silver volume dial around as far as it will go. 'Turn that rot down,' Glenda always yelled from the kitchen. But he would leave it, let it thunder through the fibro-cement walls of the house. And Gaylene would walk to the sliding aluminium framed windows and look out at the gravel road, the meatworks in the near distance, and his music and his thunder got under her skin. He would sit in a cream vinyl armchair and close his eyes, one finger tapping time on one knee.

She lets in the storm as it performs for William out there, roughly in the direction of their destination.

After the voicelessness at the pub, the heart attack, and after the Bendigo butchery was in the ground, William had taken off alone for the Northern Territory. Most of the family had a go at him over it; one of his brothers, butcher brothers, had punched him in the nose for being irresponsible, leaving Glenda and the kids behind, going bush. He had been offered a job in the butchery of a buffalo slaughterhouse in the Territory and he wanted to go. Gaylene went to the house in Bendigo, the modern brick house, for she had moved out of there long ago by that time, off with the boyfriend and the Torana car, and on this night when she walked up the driveway, past the petunias and the letterbox, there was a mud-smeared Land Rover parked behind her parents' car. The Land Rover was William's and it was packed up with jerry cans and disposal store camping gear. His friends were drinking beer around the dining table and his best mate was telling him he was mad.

William was aching for where he was going; in his mind he was already there, judging by the look on his face. She remembered that look even though she was young, a little girl, the last time she had seen it: he wore that look when he went to Papua New Guinea, when he packed shorts and singlets and work boots and the first passport he had owned. Gaylene could not understand why nobody else in the room seemed to see the look of William. Glenda was quiet. William's face had grown lined and grey since the heart attack and Gaylene thought he needed to go to the tropics, to the heat, to this place that attracted him. She wanted him to go. She urged him to go, not even thinking that this might be unfair to Glenda.

In her mind she sees herself and Brad steaming the birdsofparadise stamps from the pale-blue envelopes that William sent and putting them into a stamp album that Glenda had bought for them. Gaylene had written a letter to her father on a sheet of the tissue-like paper. In his own letters he mentioned going to the local school in the village and showing pictures of his family to the children there. A little girl had asked for his older daughter's name. In her letter Gaylene asked if the little girl could be her penfriend.

He had arrived home and she was afraid of him for a while, afraid of how much he had changed in his absence. He gave his children capes made from soft kneaded bark, bamboo spears, necklaces of cowrie shells and large seeds, grass skirts. And then he produced an envelope with the words *For my penfriend* written in dark-blue script.

The envelope was heavy. Inside she found two necklaces that William said the girl had made for Gaylene. The girl's name was Teita and she was two years older than his daughter. Gaylene could barely read that first letter with its combination of formal, almost biblical language and pidgin English. William deciphered the words, unfurling them with explanations and digressive stories. Over the years she learned to read Teita's letters by herself, reading about her school, her home, her food, her love of basketball.

William came back from Papua New Guinea with stories that never ended, stories that only slept for a time as though in the shade of jungle vines or in the cool of a white tropical mist and then emerged again throughout his life and Gaylene's life. She loved the stories and asked to hear them often, and she went on to repeat them to others.

When she was eleven she opened a letter from Teita and found a picture of a child in the envelope. On the back Teita had written: *This is my daughter, she is two years old*. William had to explain that where Teita lived it was not unusual for eleven-year-old girls to give birth to babies. Gaylene looked at the photograph of the little girl and read Teita's words again. She was in awe of Teita.

William had brought back a slide projector from his trip to Papua New Guinea. He had a set of yellow boxes filled with slides, and Teita appeared in some of them. In a sense Teita in her navy blue dress with the shirred bodice and her roman sandals came to stand at a crux between Gaylene and her father. He loved that Gaylene wrote to Teita, loved that she kept up a correspondence with a person from the other world he had brought home all those years ago. She and Teita have written sporadically over the years. Teita and her life and her place continue to loop through Gaylene's dreams. Recently she said to William that she wanted to go to Papua New Guinea to meet Teita. He smiled and said she could go only if he could go with her.

The buffalo job in the Territory did not last long and soon William moved on to Darwin, found a house in the suburb of Rapid Creek, by the beach. That was the first time he had lived near the beach in his life; theirs was an inland family, flatlands family, dirt family.

From Rapid Creek the letters and the phone calls started.

Again William wrote Gaylene letters from a tropical place, letters that appeared from a kind of dream. She had lived all her life in the state of Victoria. She had never felt tropical heat on her skin but how she had dreamed of it. How she had dreamed that she knew Teita almost as though they were sisters. How she had dreamed of walking through the white mist. And now she dreamed of walking through rainforest to see the crocodiles that William filmed with a borrowed video camera.

She never told him in the letters and phone calls about how hurt she was at that time. She did not tell him that she was living in a flat with people who did not love or even like her, that she was living with a violent man.

In Malvern she lived with the boyfriend, working part-time as a copywriter at a radio station and trying to write a book for children when the boyfriend was not looking. William was on a mission to cajole his family north. He sifted through newspapers up there, clipping job ads that he thought might suit Gaylene or Brad. In one of the letters addressed in his large square handwriting he described the local storms. He told Gaylene how he would go to the beach at night, lie on the sand, watch them come through. She hungered to know those storms just as when she was a child she had yearned to see his Papua New Guinea jungle. A job ad was enclosed in the envelope, a radio job whose requirements did not match her qualifications. Soon afterwards he phoned. 'Are you going for the job? When will you be up here?'

She told him the job was not for her and she talked

about the children's stories she was writing. He said that if she came to Darwin she could live in his house in Rapid Creek. 'I've got a garage with air-conditioning: you can sit there and write all day. I'll buy you a computer to write on. You can walk on the beach whenever you want.' She wanted that room, that computer, that place to write, that chance to walk on the beach. She wanted to see the storms and smell the wet frangipani that he mentioned sometimes. And she missed William. He sent her a self-timed picture of himself with a green tree frog perched on his beard. She sent him a Father's Day card with cartoons of lions across the front and a caption inside: *Read between the lions*. Between the lions were the words *I love you*. Her phone rang. She picked it up and heard him say with no preliminaries, 'I read between the lions.'

By then she had met Jude. He was a friend of a friend. He and the mutual friend shared a place that was twenty minutes walk from where Gaylene lived in Malvern. Several times a week she walked down Toorak Road and crossed their lawn to climb their stairs.

One day she was sitting in their kitchen with the mutual friend and she heard Jude speaking in another room. This was the first moment when the soft fine tones of his voice made her think of the word *sanctuary*. Jude's voice was like a mnemonic for what she was missing in her life, it was a reminder of calm family times when people who loved her surrounded her. In the following weeks she spent more and more time with Jude. It came as a jolt when he told her where he grew up: in the Mallee, beside the same road that she lived beside, a few towns away. The same trains had passed both their houses in the night; while she lay awake to listen and imagine boarding the trains to travel away across the paddocks, Jude had slept disturbed sleeps, sleepwalking, sweating, turning in his bed as the rumbling and tooting went by. He told her about his life, about the places and the people he loved. To the sounds of his sanctuary voice she shifted herself closer to what she had left behind. It was time to move to calmer, kinder places. She called her brother Brad and asked him for help and he said he and Nicola had just moved into a place in Brunswick and were looking for someone to live in the spare bedroom. Gaylene packed her clothes and books and writing journals and left the Malvern flat and the boyfriend and the Torana car.

Soon after she had moved in with Brad and Nicola, Jude's household disintegrated and he too moved in. Shifting to Darwin lost its appeal. The storms and the frangipani, however, would never lose their attraction as they were stored up in her with the Papua New Guinea mist and jungle, the music of Tchaikovsky, and blue-sky days by a dirt road with the meatworks looming nearby.

Jude is driving the car through Murchison and Murchison East, minutes away from Ironbark. They have caught up with the storm, driven into the storm.

The final ten minutes of driving pass swiftly, too swiftly. They pass the back reaches of the lake and the sight of it makes her ill; she feels Scott writhing in the back. This is their town, the town where their family comes from even though their immediate family has not lived here since Gaylene was two years old, years before Scott and Katy were born. They all swam in the lake as kids: Ironbark and the lake go together in their minds. Now that they see the lake they know that they have arrived in Ironbark.

Her belly churns, she feels like she is getting diarrhoea; she cannot keep her hands off her face, rubbing her skin, dragging her fingers through her long brown hair. The lake is pale and crystalline under the sheet lightning, glittering, mirroring the hundreds of dead trees, the drowned forest that pokes out of the water.

In town Jude turns right onto the road that leads to her grandparents' property. She glimpses the front of the butchery once run by Leo and Violet in the distance on the main street. Now it is run by two of William's brothers. A large sign with a cartoon of a butcher stands high above the shop: it is Brad's artwork and once the sign stood over William's butchery in Bendigo.

The cemetery is on the left. She and Brad and Marcus spent a lot of time playing in the cemetery when they were children. She knows that cemetery well, thinks of it as a kind of childhood friend.

Now she cries. She cannot hold back as they drive past the white chain-link fence. It is not just the sight of the headstones and monoliths towering over the fence that have brought on the first tears, broken her woodenness. The car is seconds away from her grandparents' house, seconds away from where she will find her mother. She has no clue as to what to say, how to act, when she sees Glenda.

The car moves into the gravel driveway, a sweep of a drive where sometimes headlights catch a mob of kangaroos crossing the back paddocks. Dark trunks, ironbarks, stand behind their backs but ahead all is lit up, every light in the house is on up there on the crest of the block. The car stops beside her grandmother's greenhouse and she sees three women and a dog standing there in the shadows in front of the blazing lights of the house. Her grandmother Violet, or Mama, stands, soft and yet solid and strong beside one of Gaylene's aunts, Yvonne, the wife of Stretch, one of William's butcher brothers. And Katy. Katy is here. Katy opens the passenger side door and puts her arms around her sister's neck for the first time since she was a baby.

4

Saturday, 2 January 1993, 10 pm

Gaylene gets out of the car and arms are all around her, cradling her, guiding her: the thin brown summery arms of Katy and the warm arms of Mama and on her back the firm touch of Yvonne. 'I love you,' Katy whispers, a caress in Gaylene's ears. 'Be strong for Mum,' Mama says, close to her, and Gaylene wants to hide in her grandmother's layers: her skirt, her petticoat. Scott has walked swiftly around the side of the house, seeking, searching. She checks that Jude is close behind and feels him press one of his hands into the small of her back, helping her sister and her grandmother and her aunt take her towards the house.

A black labrador, Max, runs in front and turns to face her, wags his long heavy tail, presses his nose into her right hand, and she feels the comfort of him; takes the chance of a moment to delay, smoothing her hand back over his head, his silken fur. Yvonne has gone inside, calling, 'Glenda, the kids are here.' The dog's fur is soft. Safe. Yet she feels Mama stiffen at her patting and she stops.

The grass close to the house is damp and gives under her feet; from the front of the house with the view across the paddocks and further out to the lake comes the wet thumping of someone else's feet. Her mother's feet.

Mum.

By now Gaylene is crying uncontrollably, sobbing as her mother flings herself at her and hugs her, saying her name over and over. Glenda is trembling and through her pale t-shirt her body feels hot and cold, giving, mother-like yet formless, without structure. Glenda is a strong woman. Although she is not as tall as Gaylene she has heavy bones and broad shoulders whereas Gaylene has the delicate bones of her father. Tonight Glenda is small and light, seeming without bones at all. Violet ushers them inside and in the foyer Leo is here, William's father, Papa. His normally lively face is looking ill and old, his eyes unable to hide the pain, and they are the liquid eyes of William and of Scott and of the sisters who stand here now. Leo kisses Gaylene. He pats Jude's shoulders and gently thanks him for what he has done.

'I panicked when you answered the phone,' he says to Gaylene. 'We didn't know how to tell you, and Scott. And we thought of Jude. But then you answered the phone.'

They move into the dining area of the kitchen, Mama and Papa's kitchen, and when Gaylene sits at the laminex table it creaks in just the same way it has always creaked since the days when she sat at this table and watched Violet taping together a doll's house of cardboard for her, or since the school holidays when she ate her lunch sitting between her then-bachelor uncles, the butchers. Now Mama makes her strong tea and sets a fine china cup in front of her on a seersucker tablecloth that looks familiar, looks like one she has seen forever.

As a child she spent a lot of time with Mama and Papa: there had not been money for expensive holidays and she and Brad had stayed here with Mama and Papa. Brad gave them those names when he was a baby. But those holidays, the holidays back when Mama and Papa had only three grandchildren, Brad, Marcus and Gaylene, the holidays were spent in another house, the old house opposite the butchery in the main street of the town. The butchers came home for their cooked lunch every day and Mama laundered butcher's coats and aprons for them to take back to work. The laminex table was there, the seersucker tablecloth was there, Gaylene sees them now in the small kitchen at the back of the house.

She cannot stop crying. Just about nobody else is crying in this noisy and chaotic room. Glenda is crying though. Glenda cries softly, quietly, almost internally. Glenda keeps up a constant weeping that Gaylene can hear through the chaos. Gaylene finds she can hardly breathe now that the weeping has begun and her mother is weeping here in this room, close, too close in time and in place: it is too soon to cope with her mother, too soon to cope with tears and words. Too soon to cope with Glenda here in the bright close light of a kitchen, Mama and Papa's kitchen.

She is ashamed. Why can she not be strong enough to look after her mother instead of being barely able to look at her, as though Gaylene is a child, a baby? Why should she not be standing up and taking care of Katy, her little sister? But Gaylene's weeping will not stop, has taken her over, blathers out of her every time she tries to speak a word, makes her hands tremble when she thinks of putting them on her mother's or her sister's arm or back or hair. After being in the house for fifteen minutes, though, she can see enough through the blathering to know that nobody here can put on an act. No matter how weak and selfish she feels, it is no good trying to pretend she is anything else at this minute. No skin, she thinks: it is like I have no skin. If Glenda has no bones, then Gaylene has no skin, no covering, nothing to hide behind or under. Flayed raw. And she looks around at everyone inside this lit-up house in the dark and each of them is the same in each of their ways. Scaffolding and props merge into the dark and rain outside, slide away into the time before any of them had heard the news.

The house is screaming out the news. William and Brad are dead.

From another room, the rumpus room, television room, her cousin Marcus appears. She has many cousins but Marcus has always been like a brother to William and Glenda's children. He is eight weeks older than her. He comes to her, stands behind her chair, rests his head on one of her shoulders, his short hair prickling her skin, and he too cries, he bawls, just like her.

'I'm sorry, I'm sorry,' Marcus says, and his voice sets into her, stays with her, a voice from a dark, thickly textured dream. 'I tried to save them, I really did.'

What does this mean? She is afraid to ask, she does not ask. She will fend off details: hold on to the waterfall story for as long as she can.

In that house in town he also spent his holidays. Gaylene hears him cry into her neck now, and in her memory she hears another cry from him, a cry from long ago, that belongs to a boy in flannelette pyjamas and a plaid dressing gown with a cord twirled around the waist. This boy came for holidays in Mama and Papa's house from further away than his cousins Gaylene and Brad. They travelled three hours across their tiny portion of north-central Victoria, sitting up in the back seat of their green car, playing I-Spy, bickering, pinching, giving Chinese burns, giggling, eating Minties for car sickness, but Marcus came from Adelaide, picked up from his mother's home by his father, Stretch, come to spend a couple of weeks with his dad and his grandparents and his cousins.

Not that this gathering of three was the happiest for Gaylene, not on the surface. She remembers the boys entertaining themselves: apart from water balloon fights and gold panning trips with Mama, Gaylene was the holiday entertainment. The two of them ganged up on her and made her cry: always easy to make her cry. She had a talking doll that asked a lot of questions. Will you be my best friend? Will you come to my party? Will you play with me? Will you come to my house? Brad and Marcus kidnapped the doll and to each of her questions they shouted no! and spat – *slagged* – on her face.

And the snails: it had taken her years to forgive them for the snails. Perhaps she does not forgive them even now. She was dressed up in her nurse's costume that Mama had made. Brad had been given Zorro and Marcus was given Batman. The boys called her to the back of the yard, behind the willow tree they all called the Faraway Tree, behind the old brown-painted shed. They said they had a bunny for her to see but when she got there she saw no bunny. Instead they had an arsenal of snails piled up, which they squashed over her, in her hair, on the nurse's apron with the embroidered red cross on the bib, onto the nurse's cap. 'All of those poor snails,' she wept to Mama as Mama bathed her afterwards.

But then there was Marcus curled up on the couch during the last days of the holidays before he was to be driven back to Adelaide, back to his mother. It was a fatly padded black vinyl couch with large round buttons, and Marcus was in his pyjamas, stayed in them all day as though he were sick, the plaid dressing gown tied snugly around him. He begged to be allowed to remain with his father. When Stretch and Mama and Papa kept saying no to that, he begged to live with Brad and her. She wanted to say yes, yes, he could come to live with them, he need not cry anymore; he could get out of the pyjamas and come to play outside, come to tease her, bully her even.

His weeping into her shoulder is loud, large. He himself has grown up loud and large and in the tears that are running down the side of her throat she can feel history, she can feel love, friendship. She feels something draining away from him: his friend, his friendship, his love for Brad is draining from him like she could put up one of her hands and catch it, let it pool in one palm and then look into it and see what Brad and Marcus shared in a wet reflection. The two of them, Brad and Marcus, have been the best of friends for all of their lives. They delight in each other; such delight is obvious to anyone who knows them. And between the three of them, if she lets herself into that picture, that reflection, she knows there is a bond of shared childhood. Marcus keeps a tiny framed picture propped on his mantelpiece. Brad, Marcus, Gaylene are in this picture, three children in technicolour, over-coloured, enclosed in a white border.

With Marcus's grief so close, in her ears, in her skin, in her head, a space opens in her, an emptiness, for maybe the only way to break this bond is through death, the death of one of them.

The phone on the kitchen wall rings. Leo answers it. He turns away from the cluster of those at the laminex table. Marcus slides into a chair. She sips tea, takes a breath, too aware of the soft urgency of Leo's voice as he speaks into the phone, leaning back against his kitchen bench. After a few minutes he hangs up and slowly turns around.

'The police?' Marcus asks.

Leo nods.

She watches his face, the quivering of his mouth, the way he can barely say the words.

'Will. They've found Will.' He leaves the room, the sound of his son's name left behind. Will.

Katy, beside her sister, cries now, softly, softly, breathing jaggedly. Jude touches one of her small hands. Gaylene cannot move, her body feels heavy, stunned, sensing through Katy's reactions the gravity, the meaning of Leo's words, even though she does not know, she does not understand any of it, and she is not sure that she wants to know or to understand, not sure that she can ever be ready to know or to understand.

She is in the dark and it is growing darker, Papa's words darken her. They've found Will; since when was Will missing, where have they found him, where was he gone, where was he missing? Dad and Brad are gone, dead, waterfalled, but where is her dad now and where has he been? And where is Brad?

Leaning close to Katy she asks, 'Do you know what happened? To Dad and Brad?'

The question sounds silly once out of her mouth but her mind is no longer straight.

'You don't know?'

She shakes her head. 'A waterfall, that's all I know.'

Katy seems to pull herself together to tell her sister the story, a story that is like a strange kind of gift, a vision, a view of what happened, a memory that could almost be shared but never quite, between sisters.

'Sort of a waterfall. A dropbar. A place where the level of the water changes and the water drops by about a metre. In the channel.'

The channel. An irrigation channel fed by the lake, a channel that runs northwest, all the way through the Mallee. A channel of thick brown water.

Katy starts to tell her. Katy knows because she was there, Gaylene's little sister was there, saw it all take place. Gaylene wants to envelop Katy, to protect her and shield her, but also to swallow her, enter her mind, see through her eyes, understand, know.

And Katy says a new word, one that Gaylene has not heard tonight, although after this night she will never again hear the word without flinching, without revisiting the vein of brown water in her mind.

Drowned.

Dad and Brad drowned.

MIDNIGHT WATER

They have not been waterfalled but drowned. She has not considered drowning until now. Somehow in her thoughts William and Brad went over the waterfall and that is where the vision ended. She has not let herself think any further than that point.

The truth seeps in, soaks in, rising, flooding: Katy's voice, so like Gaylene's own voice – they can hardly be told apart on a telephone – fills her.

A version of what happened that afternoon, a story, for the details will only ever be a story to be told and retold, heard and reheard, tries to find its level in her, rocks and quivers as though it seeks a waterline.

Death by water. This is not fair. Water is her element, water is her family's element; she sees water whenever she thinks of her family's past.

In her mind the water stories began with a tin and blue rubber backyard pool: baby Gaylene and Brad found a galah floating darkly pink on the surface. As bigger kids they crabbed barefoot down the steep red dirt walls of a reservoir. They were new in town; they knew only themselves and each other. The signs said *no swimming* but they swam: stripped to their underwear and cooled themselves in the muddy brown water, the same water that stained their bathtub with rust-brown stripes.

One spring, the first sunny day of that spring, they climbed the hill that the town liked to call the mountain or the mount, and they found a waterhole for kangaroos. The water was half a metre deep and early spring was not the time for swimming but Gaylene liked the look of the water pooled in a hollow of glittering granite scaled with mint-coloured lichen, and she pulled off her shoes and clothes while he stood watch for kids from school until he was sick of it and told her to get out. She lay on the sun-warmed granite and her hair dried stiff and green with algae.

In later years, summers, on hot hot nights, the council swimming pool stayed open late for night swimming: *night swimming, night swimming*, how she loved the cool shimmer of those words. Brad and Gaylene night swam but not together: they were teens, they were separate. The acid blue pool water was sea green under the lights on tall poles and at the bottom of the ten-feet end, the deep end, the water was black and she could not tell if her eyes were open or closed. As a family they swam in lakes, brown lakes, never blue. They slept in tents by lake foreshores; Glenda paddled thigh-deep and William swam underwater and held his breath too long for Gaylene's liking. He grabbed the kids' legs and hoisted them onto his shoulders. For a while he owned a small yacht. One day he and Scott took it out and the weather turned, a storm, and the rest of them stood on the shore in raincoats, hands sheltering brows, counting the yellow life-jacketed figures: one-two, one-two, until William took down the red sails and rowed himself and his young son back to shore. The man and the boy stepped onto the wet sand with their bare purple goose-pimpled feet and everyone in the family helped pull the wooden boat onto the grass and lash it to a tree.

Once Gaylene found a tortoise the size of a twenty-cent piece fluttering underwater at her stomach, her lycra tanksuit tummy. She scooped it up and let it tickle the palm of one of her hands. In later years, later nights, she unzipped the tent and crept through the dark to kiss boyfriends, their feet in the shallows under weeping willows, wet slippery ribbons of reeds tickling her ankles. Once the kids swam in the sea, Adelaide, holidays. Brad and Gaylene were nearly adults, they bodysurfed. *Bodysurf*: they spoke the new word to one another, the sea word. A fin cut a straight line between waves: shark, no, dolphin. Glenda said Brad *walked on water* to escape the shark-dolphin.

No matter how dry the dirt roads and paddocks and the wheat silos and the humour, her family has always found the water, found the lake, the river, the creek, the dam, the pool, the hose on the grass, the rain, the thunderstorm, the channel.

5

Saturday, 2 January 1993, 11 pm

The brown water channel has taken William and Brad.

Katy, beside her sister, gives out a strange low humming or whirring sound from deep in her throat now that she has finished telling the story, and Gaylene thinks this is what people mean by the word *keening*.

She tries to take Katy's hand but Katy gets up and says she will make more tea. More tea.

'Your hair is tangled,' she says. 'Mine was the same, earlier, because of running my hands through it. It was a mess until Mum brushed it for me. I'll brush yours. Let me brush your hair.'

Gaylene imagines the rescue workers drawing her father from the water as Katy walks away, fills a kettle, rinses a cup. He is a pale-skinned man with sparse rings of hair around his nipples. He has a beard; she has to think to be sure: for all her life William has grown beards and then shaved them off, grown them, shaved them, grown, shaved. She can never remember whether or not he has a beard but she is sure that she has heard the word *beard* whispered as the news of William's being found spreads through the house. The police do not know William personally. They must have identified him by his beard, passed on the word that a man with a beard had been removed from the water. The emergency workers must take care of him, she wants to make the scene as it should be: the workers lift him gently, hold on to his long limbs, not letting them drag on the ground, not letting the stony bank mar his skin, mark him, hurt him. The ground: that stony ground, sharp with quartz, golden with clay, glittering with mica, this is the soil of her childhood, the soil she imagines crumbling between her fingers whenever she thinks of her sense of landscape, place, home.

More words are going around the house. She hears a fresh burble of news that has come with the phone call from the police. Leo walks back into the room. He comes to the table where Gaylene sits, Jude holding one of her hands in both of his own.

'The search has been called off for the night. The storm. Too dangerous for the police divers. They'll find Brad tomorrow.'

Brad is still in the water. He will spend the night in the channel. The news strikes her as the worst so far. Life, death, these are ideas she cannot comprehend tonight, the reality of the words will not sink in. But the word *drowning* sinks in. And Brad in the water, left to drift in the dark, in the storm: that sinks in.

She tries to bring him close. Brad in their parents' house in Northcote. That was maybe three weeks ago, not long before Christmas. He was asleep on the brown tweed couch. His dog, a bitser named Bucket, for reasons known only to Brad and his girlfriend, was beside him, a tight smooth coil under one of Brad's arms. Brad was wearing a pale-blue chambray shirt, pale-blue denim jeans. His hair is short and dark blond. He has green-blue eyes like Glenda's but they were closed. He was tired; he had been working extra hours at the video shop, supporting himself, working on his drawings in the hours around the edges of the shifts. And his girlfriend, Nicola, had left him. He was in hospital with pneumonia a few weeks earlier. Gaylene and Jude went to visit him. Tubes up his nose, a cannula in the back of one hand, both hands bruised where the nurses changed the needle from hand to hand each morning; a cough that made it hard for him to talk. He was pale. She worried about him. She and Jude stayed for a while and then he was too tired and he said between coughs that he wanted to half-doze in front of one of the videos that Marcus had dropped off from the shop where they worked. And then a few days later, there he was at Elm Street, sleeping on the tweed couch in his chambray shirt.

Now if she could just think him from the tweed couch to the bed of the channel, still in the chambray and the denim, sleeping, perhaps dreaming, if she could picture him there, then perhaps she could see where he was, she could find him.

She wants him out of the water.

Everyone in the house wants him out of the water but they know the police must cease their work tonight. The storm has stopped them, the same storm she had appreciated on the drive here. Thunderstorm. Tchaikovsky storm.

Katy comes back, puts tea on the table in front of her sister, in front of Jude. Gaylene asks why she is not having tea. 'When I first came here, back to the house, from the channel,' Katy says, 'I could not stop drinking tea. I needed it to calm me. To warm me. You need the tea now.'

To her sister Katy looks settled and strong. She even looks taller, grown up sky-high, hovering, untouchable. 'I will look after you. I need a job to do.' She goes back to the kitchen bench and picks up a hairbrush with a velvet scrunchie looped over its handle and comes to sit beside her sister's chair.

She brushes Gaylene's gnarled hair, for Gaylene has not noticed before now that she has been running her hands through her hair, worrying it, twisting it: her hair is as tangled as reeds. Katy brushes, knowing long hair, knowing the family texture of their hair. And the brushing reminds Gaylene of when her sister scratched her back when they were younger and shared a blue-painted bedroom with twin beds; Gaylene was afraid of the dark, afraid of the violent dreams she knew she would have as soon as she fell asleep, and she would coax Katy to climb into her bed, slip under the dark-blue maple leaf patterned bedspread, and scratch her back. Katy diligently followed the whispered instructions: scratch, rub, round in a circle, up and down, side to side, writing messages on her back that Gaylene had to guess; as the big sister Gaylene could get away with this and she knew those nights had a cruel edge, even an abusive taint, but the scratching soothed her fear of the dark. Sometimes the back-scratching seemed to stop the bad dreams from coming.

Katy brushes, starting near the ends, untangling it section by section, using her other hand to hold the hair away a little from the scalp so that it does not pull and hurt. She works gradually upwards until her sister's hair is smooth and then she keeps brushing even though the tangles are gone. Through her hair Gaylene feels the tremor in Katy's hands. The brushing feels good. She does not want it to stop. It reminds her that she has a body: she exists.

As children both sisters had been like slender ragged flowers. Now Gaylene has fleshed out but Katy has not. She is still a teenager. And at this moment Katy's skin looks as thin as bruised petals.

Tonight the two of them are truly bonded as sisters and the years before fall away like the softest of paper walls. Gaylene looks at her sister, sees beyond the child-like stature and admires Katy's strength and determination to keep walking, keep going, even after what she has seen. The hurt shines through: Gaylene sees it in the colours forming under her sister's eyes; the skin seems to have thinned out as though all she has seen today is weighing down her vision, has etched itself under her skin, under her eyes, embedded it into a mauve parchment. Gaylene thinks of irises, the purple of irises, the petals, the papery sheath at the base of the flower. What Katy saw is encased in iris parchment.

Through the glass doors near the laminex table Gaylene sees the dog Max walking across the lawn and then lying down by the doors, fur pressed against the glass, head on his front paws. The memory of a recent incident nags at her, a dog incident, a dog accident. She turns abruptly to Katy, reaching up to stop the hairbrush.

'Bucket,' she says.

Katy nods. 'I know.'

Two weeks ago Brad's black bitser dog, Bucket, disappeared. Gaylene found out when she went to Elm Street for Sunday night dinner; in the kitchen she stood with her mother while Glenda served up the roast meat and vegetables. 'Did you hear Bucket's missing?' Glenda said.

'Permanently missing,' Brad's voice came from behind his sister. He walked into the kitchen and she looked at him and he could barely meet her gaze. 'She drowned,' he said. He told the story: his newly ex-girlfriend had come to take the dog out with her for the day. Her new boyfriend went walking with Bucket by the Yarra River. They were at Dight's Falls, a low waterfall amidst rocks and concrete pipes, and Bucket chased a bird into the water and went under and did not come up again. Brad had gone down there every day for a week, searching for any trace of her. He put up fliers on telephone poles, seeking information. Bucket never turned up.

Lately Gaylene has been thinking how much Brad has lost. Too much. Years have passed since he finished his graphic design degree and his illustrations and cartoons are piling up in his folios and on his heavy drawing desk but no jobs come his way. Just before Gaylene and Jude moved out of Brunswick, one of Brad's beloved tabby cats went missing and never returned. He has lost his girlfriend. He has been sick, in hospital. His dog has drowned. Bucket. Bucky. Too much.

The black fur against the glass starts to blur in her vision as she hears her mother's soft murmur of weeping again; she turns from the glass, from the dog, and traces Glenda's steps for a few minutes as she drifts from room to room and person to person. Gaylene senses the hunger in her, the desperation for all of this to stop, for none of it to be happening. But she is looking at her mother's back and her side, turning away when Glenda looks in her direction. Gaylene cannot yet look directly at Glenda. They have not been close to one another for a long time, perhaps ever. Gaylene was close to William. And then she was close to none of them for a while and the pieces have only just started to come together again and she cannot pretend now that she and Glenda are close. She feels too young, she feels too old, to cope with her mother's pain. But the time when she will have to face it is moving near.

Glenda and William's best friends who still live in the Bendigo street with its lush lawns and petunia beds run from the front door to meet Glenda in the middle of the kitchen. They are dressed up for they have come from a wedding reception. They wrap their arms around Glenda and then they come to kiss Gaylene and she wants the man of the couple to stay close for he makes William feel nearby all of a sudden.

As they and other people arrive many of them tell stories of how and where they heard the news. These people are in shock, they are babbling. Someone thought it was this person who was dead or that person. On hearing the news each seemed to have contracted the tragedy around themselves, immediately thinking of their most dreaded or seemingly likely losses: mother, father, child, sibling.

The sisters sit at the table, close and quiet, nodding, murmuring, as these tales are told. They have no such tales. For them it is the worst; it is the close family they have lost. Father and brother.

And Glenda, their mother, has the greatest loss and although the sisters sense it they cannot know it well enough, know what it is to lose a husband and a child, husband or a child. They do not have husbands or children.

Glenda sits down heavily opposite Gaylene at the table. Glenda fiddles with her clothing, the striped grey and white t-shirt that already looks too big for her, as though she has lost weight, lost her substance, her stuffing. Her eyes are glazed and look unfathomable. Her eldest daughter clasps her hands around another cup of tea that has appeared in front of her.

Rosemary and her family arrive. Rosemary is William's sister. Her husband comes in first and Glenda looks past him for Rosemary. Everyone knows she is afraid to enter: gentle, kind Rosemary, who has given them all much love in the years since she was a bridesmaid at William and Glenda's wedding in a pink empire-line dress, frangipani in her hair. She appears and almost falls to her knees at the sight of her sister-in-law. 'Oh, Glenda,' she says. The two women walk away, disappear into the lounge room, arms around one another.

Gaylene turns to her sister. Katy tells her how their mother heard the news of what happened at the channel.

6

Saturday, 2 January 1993, midnight

The sisters are reflected in the glass doors. Katy's voice is quiet enough for only Gaylene and Jude to hear.

'Stretch drove Marcus and me back here, from the channel. We waited in his car while he went in to tell Mama and Papa. He says he went in and found them watching the cricket on television, and he turned it off and stood in front of the TV, and, laughing, they asked what he was doing. He said he had very bad news. William and Brad were gone and they were not coming back. He explained, and then he went to get Marcus and me. We talked about how Mum would be told. Papa wanted to tell her. He drove off in his car. The rest of us sat here, and we waited.'

Gaylene pieces together the story from Katy's words and later from Papa and from Glenda.

Glenda was sitting in a deckchair at Bushy's, reading a book. She had been visiting old friends of her family not far from Bushy's. As she drove back to the block she heard sirens, ambulances, and wondered if there had been a road accident. Later she heard a car on the dirt track, wondered who it could be: it sounded like Leo's car but it was going too fast. He never drives fast. Ever since he bought the new car, the silver Telstar, he has driven more slowly, carefully, not wanting to put a mark on the car and perhaps being afraid of the quiet way the car has of picking up speed. The car pulled up, in sight now. It was Leo. Without knowing why, Glenda lay down her book and put her hands over her ears and closed her eyes.

'Whatever it is, Leo,' she said, 'don't tell me. I just don't want to know.'

But he had to tell her. And he did. He had to help her to the car. They passed the slaughteryards, drove up his driveway, and when they got to his house he almost had to carry her inside.

Katy sighs, slowly, loudly, as she tells her sister about Papa bringing Glenda into the house where she and Marcus waited with Mama. 'I could hear her before she came through the front door. She was saying "It just can't be true. It can't be. Not Brad. Not Brad." And I was selfish, hurt, because I thought she was saying it should have been one of us instead of Brad. She was always so close to Brad.'

It is true. Glenda adores Brad. Perhaps she adores him the most of her children. Gaylene has never envied the love between them. She has had little reason: these matters often sort themselves out in families. Her father adores her.

More people flow into the house. Katy breaks away. Her new boyfriend has arrived, come with a friend, and they are soon followed by other friends. The friends enfold Katy and she disappears with them.

Glenda passes, going to sit on a couch in the rumpus room, the couch at the back of the room, from where she can see Gaylene; she keeps turning her head to look at her, as though she thinks her daughter may go somewhere, dissipate into air.

Gaylene makes herself get up and go to Glenda but as she perches herself on the edge of a couch cushion she can think of no words to say. She tells Glenda just that.

'There are no words,' Glenda says.

Glenda's voice is gentle and loving, perhaps more loving than ever before. Gaylene is shocked; somehow she had expected Glenda to be cold and distant when speaking to the ones left behind, the ones left when Brad is gone.

Glenda keeps talking, saying, 'Don't let them drug me up. I heard some of them whispering about sedating me. You don't let them. All right? I won't sit here ga-ga and out of it while Brad's out there in the channel.'

Gaylene nods. She agrees that the last thing Glenda needs is to be sedated. But she cannot touch Glenda's pain; she has never been able to touch Glenda's pain.

Around the rumpus room she sees Mama's crocheted doilies on every surface, including the chair arms and backs and under vases of flowers from the garden. She looks up at the seventies and eighties family photos on the walls. This house is on the same dirt road as the old house where Glenda's ancestors first settled but also where Glenda lived for a time as a young woman. That was a few years after Glenda lost her own mother in a house fire. Gaylene has heard the story of Glenda's mother's death many times since childhood. Maybe she knew the story before she was old enough to remember being told as for most of her life she has been afraid of fire. (*But water. Gaylene has never ever been afraid of water.*) In the past Glenda joked darkly about the long list of tragic sudden deaths in her family history. She spoke of rumours that the family is cursed, rumours handed down from Millicent, Glenda's grandmother, who had once lived at Bushy's. 'We must've upset some bugger along the way,' Glenda would say, an ironic lilt in her voice, a lilt that mimicked Millicent's voice.

Glenda was thirteen the night her mother died. Glenda was asleep in her bed in the house her family lived in, in a town on the Murray River. She woke to find the end of her bed on fire and a neighbour at her window. Two men helped her to climb out and as she climbed she heard Agnes calling from inside the house, inside the flames. 'Look after David,' she called. Glenda thought her mother must have forgotten that her little brother David was staying with their grandmother that night. But later she thought that Agnes knew she would not get out of the fire alive and meant that Glenda should look after David once Agnes was gone. 'Call your father,' the men shouted, and she ran down to the post office in her nightie and bare feet. She had never before called her father at his work, at the newly built RSL club, but somehow she called the right number and her father, Digger, never answered the phone at the club but there he was on the end of the line that night.

The house burnt to the ground. Agnes' body was not severely marked, not burned: she died from smoke inhalation. Thirteen-year-old Glenda saw pictures of her at the inquest: she leant over slightly to view the fan of black and white photographs on the coroner's desk and the images of her dead but not charred mother seeped into her and stayed forever.

Later she would speak of Agnes to her own children, but still they know little of Agnes except her name, her face in wartime-brown photographs, and that she died in a burned-down house when their mother was a child.

Glenda's children could reel off the story of Agnes and the fire but Gaylene was often to think that none of them could truly look at Glenda and recognise that motherless child, burned-mother child in her. Not then. Not when they were children gathered around her and her photographs, her and the marquisite watch that had once been worn by Agnes and that she took out of a lace-edged box to show them now and then.

Tonight the burned-mother child is not far away; Gaylene can almost smell the fire, the water, the fear in Glenda. And Gaylene is wordless, useless, around her mother even at the best of times. When did she start to feel this way, she asks herself, and she thinks of her adolescence in the Mallee and the moment when she felt herself come adrift from her family.

It is true that Gaylene was always closer to William than to Glenda but in the past her relationship with Glenda had been warm. The years in the Mallee had turned it around. She had hated living there, hated the dryness as she grew up and began to look around at the landscape and to feel the climate that she lived in. She was unpopular at school and spent a lot of time alone in a pink spare bedroom that her parents had allowed her to have, Katy left with the blue room and the twin beds. The pink room was at the front of the house, facing the highway, facing the railway line that split the highway in two. She read books and she wrote in a heart-patterned diary, a *Sweet Dreams* diary.

She stopped wanting to talk to her family, who all seemed happy enough in the town when she wanted to escape to a place with hills and proximity to the sea, a place where silver silos were replaced with lighthouses sweeping beams out over water; she wanted to leave but the family stayed and in her mind she left them instead of, or as well as, the town.

And then came the time when her gradual drifting

turned into a swift swim in the opposite direction to her family; the drifting culminated in an event that she thinks of almost every day, an event that she still writes about in the diaries that she has continued to keep since that period in her life.

Gaylene, aged sixteen, in a thin denim jacket, was at an ocean beach facing Bass Strait. She had never known such wind. Her hair stood on end. She was a skinny girl: all through high school she had been taunted for having the figure of a rake. She moved down the boardwalk, hearing the timber under her feet and the roaring of the waves below. The lighthouse on her right was phosphorescently white against a stormy afternoon sky and she found herself looking up at it again and again. She left the boardwalk, lagging behind the people who were there with her, a group of women and girls. She found a large, sturdy egg-shaped boulder on the shore. She sat on it and around her she saw thousands of water-smoothed black pebbles and she listened to them hum and roll with the waves. Her wrists and hands were blue with cold but the denim sleeves would not pull down any further. The hum and roll drew her in as the other people moved out of her sight around to the more treacherous rocks and blowholes. Her egg-shaped boulder was unmoving among the pebbles even when the seafoam crept up to lace its curved underside.

Where Gaylene lived in the Mallee there were no lighthouses except for the lighthouse images that from that day she would fuse onto the shining silver wheat silos and the lone twinkling light, a warning light for aircraft, at the top of the hillock on the edge of her town.

The ocean lighthouse watched her. It appeared to know what she already knew, even though she did not yet have proof of what she knew. Inside the sixteen-year-old Gaylene in her thin denim jacket there was the first trace of a baby.

In her suitcase, for she was on a holiday, a school camp, she had hidden a cardboard box. It contained a pregnancy kit that she bought at a chemist in the town near the beach. She will sneak it home and she will do the test. She planned it as she left the lighthouse that day and cast a look backwards, lingering on the shining white tower; she will do the test while her parents are at work, will do it in her bedroom, and then she will pack the contents of the box into a bag and take the bag to the public park across the road and dispose of it in a bin.

Gaylene had never doubted that a baby was inside her since the moment of conception. She was pregnant and she loved it. The love was not like that of a mother who believes that she will follow through with the pregnancy. She knew that this pregnancy would end abruptly at some point in the near future. But still she loved the feeling inside her. She loved the warmth, the glow, and she will not forget it.

This girl in her thin denim jacket already knew that the town she lived in had become dangerous. Small towns, she told herself, can and do kill girls like her. She listened to the waves crash, not exactly without fear but without moving away. She sat on the rock and looked out to sea and felt older than her own parents; older than her mum, who still imagined her a child; older than her dad, in whose eyes she wanted to remain perfect. The wind caught the flaps of her denim jacket. Her hair was flying, the colours of the sky and the sea whipping through it as she got to her feet and began the ascent up the side of the cliff.

The lighthouse went with Gaylene back to the Mallee. She sensed distance in herself, waves in her ears, seagulls' calls in her mind. She did the pregnancy test. She weed in the tiny test tube and put it in its brown plastic stand. William and Glenda were at the butchery. Gaylene's brothers and sister were in a different world from her that day: their voices were far away. She checked the plastic indicator and saw the positive result. She hid the test equipment in a paper bag. She lay under her quilt, the flesh-pink quilt that had once been her great-grandmother's, and she cried for a while. Following the plan thought up with the lighthouse looking out over her, she got up and went to the park across the road. She walked past the cockatoos and galahs in the big domed aviary – *dance, cocky, dance*, the town children liked to call as they passed – and she dropped the bits and pieces of the test in different bins around the park.

The diary that Gaylene liked to write in, the heart-patterned *Sweet Dreams* diary, was no longer safe. She knew that Glenda read it sometimes. She did not write about the pregnancy, about the pink glow inside her.

But Glenda guessed. In a drawer, Gaylene had a packet of contraceptive pills, ostensibly for period pain, to start taking with her next period. When she got her first period at the age of thirteen, she noticed that Glenda had marked the family calendar that hung in the kitchen, their own butchery calendar, with a tiny G for Gaylene in red pen. The G was marked on the days when her period was due. Perhaps Glenda had kept counting with her red G marking every month in her head or in her own diary. Or else she had been snooping in the drawer, observing the packet of pills as it remained unopened. Or perhaps she knew *as a mother knows*, for those were the words that William would soon use about the situation. In any case Glenda knew the truth.

Glenda asked questions: When's your period due? Did your period come yet?

And Gaylene answered, eyes averted: In a week or two. It's not due yet. I don't know. I lose track. It's not regular.

William asked the biggest question in the end. Dad wants to talk to you, Glenda said, standing on the threshold of her daughter's bedroom. Her voice trembled and Gaylene heard the tremble but pretended not to notice; she put on a false smile, she tried to make a joke, tried to say that she had homework, but Glenda was not having any of it.

In the kitchen William's demeanour was different to Glenda's. Gaylene, in her pyjamas, was sad to find that she pitied him a little. He did not believe that she was pregnant. He even said so, to begin. Softly he said her name, he looked into her eyes and spoke. Mum thinks you're pregnant. Gaylene laughed. She felt herself acting, felt him believing in her character, her role. She laughed like this talk was embarrassing and she could not believe the words she was hearing. William laughed too. He went along with the routine that Gaylene carried out for him. He said, Mum thinks she knows as a mother knows. But I don't think you're pregnant. I think you're happy, happier than I've seen you in a long time.

He was right in some ways. She was happy. She had a vision of a lighthouse that looked out over an ocean, like a house with a view in the opposite direction to the Mallee, to this town that she hated. And then there was the happiness of the pink glow, the baby, and that happiness helped her to know that she had boundaries, she had privacy, she had her own private house, lighthouse, inside her. William said he had to ask her if it was true. Was she pregnant? She put a gently sarcastic, teasing, flirting note into her actor voice, liar voice, and she said no. Her father hugged her. She was limp in his arms, his arms around her and around the pink glow inside her.

The girl in the pyjamas, the girl with blonde-tipped brown hair and little girl freckles, lied to her father. That was a first.

She knew the late period was not going to arrive but still she waited for the flow of her sixteen-year-old life to carry her where it would. Glenda grew bolder with her questions. Every night Gaylene dried the dishes at the sink and she tried on that cute routine: she laughed, she joked, she talked to Glenda considerably more than she had been known to talk to her in recent times. In her school uniform Gaylene dried each plate, skipping her voice along to talk about homework and school plays and friends. Glenda did not smile.

Drifting with the flow ended abruptly. Glenda made an appointment with a doctor, a doctor who once saved Glenda's life, a doctor who trampled her daughter. When it came time for them to move from the waiting room to the surgery, Gaylene said no as Glenda got to her feet. I will go by myself, she said. Her voice was quiet and strong, recalling the lighthouse on the cliff. She sat under fluorescent tubes in a cold room and the doctor said he was going to do a test. She heard the words, hated the words, knew enough, small town girl or not, to know that this doctor was doing what he had no right to do. She was sixteen. She was no child. She did not have to be there. She could not be ordered to have a pregnancy test even at her mother's request. And she knew already that whatever was to happen from there on, this doctor would not be part of it. He would not touch her.

She spoke up in her lighthouse voice. I do not need a test. I did a home test. I am pregnant. He asked when she did the test and the date of her last period. Then he left the room without another word. When he returned twenty long minutes later, Glenda was with him. He had told her the news. They had already made an appointment with an abortion clinic. For the time being she let it wash over her. As they left the surgery the doctor tried to stroke the back of her hair and she ducked away from his touch. He and Glenda exchanged looks, shakes of their heads.

In the car Glenda put her hand on top of her daughter's hand. She told Gaylene that she loved her, her voice breaking with the difficulty of it. It had been years since she had said those words to her daughter, years since Gaylene allowed her to say the words. Now Gaylene would still not allow it, although she did hear it; it did seep through the layers, not that you would have known it to look at her face. She pulled her hand away. She pushed a cassette tape into the car's player. She turned her head to stare through the window.

The day before the abortion she lay on a bench at school, sick, nauseous. An English teacher, a kind woman, came to ask if she was all right. Gaylene wanted to tell her, wanted this teacher to fold her into a hug, make her not feel sick with the lies and with the life inside.

William and his daughter never spoke about the pregnancy or the abortion. She was ashamed to look at him. On the day her mother drove her to the city for the abortion, Glenda said that William wanted to come but that he had nobody to mind the butchery. The butcher was left to stand at his block, chopping meat, lies falling about him in the sawdust, for she had indeed lied to him and she knew he was shocked, knew this from the way he did not say a word, did not question, did not comment. He was hurting.

All the way to the city she was sick and Glenda kept having to pull over so that her daughter could vomit.

In the clinic Glenda stepped forward to sign the

form. But the receptionist looked past her and handed it to Gaylene. At least in this clinic, in the city, she was sixteen, she was responsible for her own body, her own baby. She signed. Glenda kissed her and Gaylene began to cry.

Soon she was wearing only a cloth gown and her feet were in metal stirrups pulled up high above her. She was sobbing loudly. Someone said she was a bit young. And then the anaesthetic sent her to sleep and while she slept the pink glow dimmed and faded to a faint glimmer, a memory-glimmer. Afterwards she woke with cramps in her abdomen and a pad between her legs. In a room full of dazed-looking women she drank tea with milk and ate teddy bear biscuits. She had not often drunk tea before this day. She discovered that tea is warm and comforting, even more so when drunk in the company of other women. She sat back in her chair and took her time with her tea and her time with the women.

Since the day at the lighthouse Gaylene imagined herself standing aloft with packed bags. These were not like the sad floppy schoolbag that she carried to school each day. The bags were smart brown leather suitcases. She looked out over the paddocks and even over the tops of the silver silos. She did not notice that the thinness of her body mimicked a teetering white tower. She cared only to look at the view outside herself. She was looking out to sea.

Gaylene knows she has carried the abortion and the day at the lighthouse with her ever since, and it has taken years to find her way back to her family. But tonight she feels no closer to Glenda than when she was her teenage self, her Mallee self, and then her lighthouse self.

7

Sunday, 3 January 1993, 1 am

Glenda seems to want to be near Gaylene. Perhaps it is just that she wants her children close. That is what she told Jude all those hours ago, kilometres ago, worlds ago. Gaylene starts to think. She does know what it is to love William and Brad. Everyone in this house with the family landscapes surrounding it – the lake out the front, the slaughteryards a short distance along the road, Bushy's a little further, the family butchery in town – knows what it is to love William and Brad. Each of them knows it differently but they know it.

She puts her hand on one of Glenda's bare wrists. Glenda takes her hand immediately. They talk of Brad out in the channel, out in the night, and of William, already found, lying silently somewhere else.

What must her mother think, Gaylene wonders as the words pass between them. Is she remembering, is she meeting them both again for the first time, marrying her husband, giving birth to her son, here, tonight, in her mind? The resonances of those events must be stored in nearby places, along this dirt road outside, in at the bush nursing hospital in town, even in Gaylene herself, for she knows these memories, knows these stories. She herself is picking up the traces and telling pieces of the family stories to herself right now as she talks softly with her mother.

After Agnes's death and after Glenda had finished her schooling she stayed at Bushy's for a time. Every couple of days William would come along the dirt road, driving lambs to his family slaughteryards, the lambs whose throats he would cut. She would see him coming and lean on the gate at Bushy's to wait for him. They were courting. Leo could not wait for them to get married so that he could get some work out of

Will. Gaylene thinks of her parents' wedding pictures: large glossy coloured photographs, Glenda in ivory satin, William in a Beatles suit with drainpipe trousers. He is nineteen. She is eighteen. They are pictured pulling a wishbone. Not very long after the wedding, Brad will be born and Glenda will form a bond with him that is fast and strong.

While someone comes to speak to Glenda, Gaylene slips outside for a moment, breathes the stormy air. And she finds Max, the dog still lying on his stomach, body pressed in against the house, against the glass. He sleeps. Yet his legs are working furiously underneath him, pumping, paddling. Swimming. Whimpers come from deep inside him.

Now she knows what happened at the channel; now the story rests uneasily in her thoughts. Like Katy, Max played a part. Max was at the channel.

She wants to hold on to his fat sleek body, hold on to him tightly. She picks up one long floppy ear and whispers to him that it is not his fault. *It is not your fault*. She puts her arms around his body, feels the warmth, but also the cold in him, for he is shivering.

She holds him: Max is cold, Max is shivering, Max is dreaming, Max is swimming.

Max is Toby's dog, her eldest brother's dog.

'Does Toby know? Toby and Jess?' she asks Glenda through the half-open glass doors behind her, where Glenda has come to stand. Glenda shakes her head. 'We thought about it,' she says. 'About tracking them down – I think they're due to be somewhere in Malaysia now. But if we found them, and if they could get a flight home, they would always remember that their honeymoon was cut short by this news. I don't want their honeymoon to be like that.'

A part of Gaylene agrees with Glenda but she is shocked that Toby and Jess will go on holidaying, honeymooning, not knowing that William and Brad are gone. They will miss the funeral. *The funeral, she cannot imagine what the funeral will be like*. She has only known Toby, only known of his existence, for nine months, but he is family, he is one of them, he is her brother, Glenda's son, and she wishes he could be here. She wants Toby close by.

Toby is two and a half years older than Brad and a

little over four years older than Gaylene. To her Toby looks like a young version of Glenda's late father, Digger.

Nine months ago she did not know that she had another brother, that before Glenda was married she had given birth to a first child, first boy. Gaylene had grown up with no awareness of this brother, this sibling who had lived a kind of parallel life with his adoptive family in Melbourne while Glenda and William and their children traversed a line through the flatlands of country Victoria. She never knew about him; she wishes she had known about him. But Glenda said it would have been worse if she had known, or if any of them had known apart from her and William: 'The years were hard enough for me,' she said. 'Missing him. It would have been too sad for you to know you had this brother that you could not meet.'

Glenda told the story of the birth of her first child in late March 1992, when she had a phone call from the adoption agency she had registered with a few years earlier: they had contacted her son and he wished to meet her.

Remembering, Gaylene hears her mother, emotion heaving in her voice, saying, 'You have a brother that you don't know about.' Gaylene laughed nervously. A brother. 'He's four years older than you. Born in 1965. When I was sixteen.'

The story tumbled out over the following moments, days, months. After the death of Glenda's mother, Glenda lived between homes: between her two grandmothers, one in a town on the Murray River, the other at Bushy's, and between boarding school and home with her brother David and with Digger, who had lost the plot as a dad after the fire that choked the life from Agnes.

At sixteen Glenda fell pregnant to a boy in town. They talked of marriage but his family would not allow it and she was sent to a Catholic maternity home in Melbourne for the duration of the pregnancy – the confinement, as her daughter thinks of it, her mother confined, hidden. Glenda remembered the lectures, the glares, the moralising from the nuns; the only empathy to be found was shared among the swollen-bellied teenage girls.

Glenda gave birth to a boy. She told the nuns she had changed her mind: she would keep the baby.

'They wouldn't have a bar of it,' Glenda said to Gaylene all those years later when she told the story. 'They took him away when I was asleep. I didn't get to say goodbye. They said that was for the best.'

Did not get to say goodbye: the memory of these words haunt Gaylene. Today another of Glenda's sons has been taken and nobody has said goodbye. A baby was in a crib one moment, then followed a void of twenty-six years with no transition, no ceremony, no ritual; and now a son, a brother, has been smiling one moment, playing a song on a cassette player, and then in another moment he was swallowed by a body of water.

Glenda met William not long after the first baby had gone and they married in the church on the hill at one end of Ironbark on the way out to the original goldmining settlement. Glenda told William about her baby and the two of them worked to try to reclaim him, to see if they could get him back. The laws were fast and firm. They had no hope of getting the baby back. With her new baby in her belly, William's baby, Glenda prepared to wait out the years until the first child was of age and she could meet him again. She knew she would see him again. She and William chose the names Bradley William for their new baby and then they decided to add a third name, the name Glenda had given the baby who was adopted. Unknowingly, with this third name Brad held onto the memory of the older brother he had never met. He was sweet to his mother. He soothed her.

She went to the agency to meet her grown-up first son. They got along and he ended up going to Elm Street with Glenda, pulling up near the fence, getting out and walking through the gateway with her. Later Glenda said she saw William through the bay window, tidying up, straightening his shirt, hurrying about after seeing them out the front. Her son Toby met William and Scott and Katy. Glenda decided to call Brad over in Brunswick, have him come around to meet his brother. She did not seem to think to call her elder daughter, perhaps because Gaylene was on the other side of the city, or perhaps Glenda was thinking of times past when Gaylene could not be trusted to come over if she was called.

Gaylene met Toby three nights later. Toby came to Elm Street in jeans and a brown suede jacket, bringing his fiancée, Jess. The family members sat around the dining table under the dead people and got to know one another. Gaylene was flushed, nervous. She liked Toby from the first moment, although it was disconcerting that he looked like her mother and like Digger. Toby's eyebrows are just like Glenda's and looking at them made her think that she was talking to Glenda. And she was not entirely comfortable looking into Glenda's face. But she was getting there.

Pregnant. At sixteen. Glenda. This new knowledge touched her in a soft, haunted place inside.

And several months later the family piled into a church for Toby and Jess's wedding; the wedding was by the sea and Jess got out of her father's MG in a Victorian cream silk dress, a dark pink Asiatic lily pinned in her swept-up hair. Toby wanted all of the family there although they felt awkward, numerous: there are six in the family, seven including Jude. It was the first time they had dressed up and all gone out together since the kids had grown to adults, and certainly the first time that Toby had also been present. She thought her mother looked beautiful in a satiny teal-coloured outfit.

Gaylene wanted the day to be smooth for Toby: she tried to be subtle, looking around, saying hello to Toby's friends, most of whom he had known since primary school. She was his sister but she was new to his life and his friends.

At the reception William and Jude sat at the corner of a table by large windows with a view of Half Moon Bay, the HMAS *Cerberus*'s rust glowing as the sun set and the last of the wedding photographs were taken on the pier. She stood with her mother and Katy. Luckily the music was getting louder for she was running out of things to say.

Her gaze kept sliding over to William and Jude as she tried to implore Jude to come and talk with her, dance with her, perhaps they could take a walk on the pier now that Toby and Jess and the rest of the wedding party were back inside, rubbing the cold from their arms. He was not looking at her. He was deep in conversation with her father. This went on for more than an hour and she noticed that Glenda too was looking in their direction, trying to catch William's attention.

Brad wafted in and out of the room. He had a bad cold; it was almost summer yet he wore a woollen sports jacket and he could not get warm. At one point he picked up Gaylene's hand and put it on his forehead. He was sweating, boiling hot. It shocked her: the holding of her hand in his, the heat of his skin, the damp sweat. She could not remember being so physically close to him since their childhood. Despite the sweating he had to keep going outside to sit in his car, turning up the heater as high as it would go, trying to warm himself, and then he would come back inside to be sociable. Midway through the evening he had to give up, say goodnight, and go home. In fact he went to Elm Street, maybe sensing that he should not be alone that night. When Glenda and William went home later in the night they would find him delirious, murmuring in his sleep, and the next day he would be admitted to Fairfield Hospital with pneumonia.

She saw William lean over to hug Jude. Glenda saw it too and looked confused. The two men got up to come over to the women. William had a huge smile on his face and he hugged her when he reached her. She pretended to laugh it off but he did not seem to care. He held on even as she tried to shrug herself away.

She took the walk on the pier with Jude and she asked what he and William had been talking about.

'You. I told him how much you love him.'

She was annoyed but was not sure why.

'He said he knows we will marry one another one day.'

She liked that but still she was embarrassed. The last few years of hiding, of going underground from her parents, her family, had not quite worn off. She loved them but speaking the words, having them spoken for her, did not feel right. She still needed to have her secrets, her privacy, the house inside her, the lighthouse.

They went inside. They danced and William and Glenda stood at the edge of the dance floor and watched them, their heads close together. Her father kept looking at her as she tried to avoid his gaze. He said something to Glenda and Glenda laughed, shook her head; he nudged her, took her arm and tugged and she relented. They walked onto the dance floor and for a few minutes they danced beside Gaylene and her boyfriend.

Now Gaylene turns to Jude who has come to sit close to her, crouching on the floor in the rumpus room, stroking her ankles. 'Thanks for telling Dad that I love him,' she says.

'He already knew,' he says, 'but he loved hearing the words, just the same.'

# 8

Sunday, 3 January 1993, 2 am

Her eyes are filmed like the glass of a lighthouse on a night when the rain will not let up.

Brad. It has been two years since she and Jude shared the house in Brunswick with Brad and Nicola. At first Jude had slept on Brad's couch out by the white marble fireplace. After he moved in to her bedroom to share her bed, it was like having a best friend to whisper to at night. It was a long time before they became lovers. They stayed awake late and talked by the light that came in through the one sash window, continuing the long conversations they had started before he had come to stay. Next door a household of Goths resided. They came out at night, one of them revving an old car on blocks by a row of sallow corn stalks in his back yard at two, three, four am. Somehow they grew to love the sound of the Goth driving the car that went nowhere as they lay there unable to sleep until the Goth gave it up for the night.

During the days while Jude and Nicola were at work, Gaylene and Brad did their own work at his large heavy desk at the back of the house. A rectangular window looked out to a fig tree with its dark green splayed leaves; with that cool view in front of him Brad would lay out his tins of pens and pencils and his tubes of paint and work on a folio of cartoons and illustrations as she wrote, working on the children's book that she had almost been enticed to go to Darwin to write.

Bucket the bitser dog snored at Brad's feet; the cats sat together like window ornaments on the table in the sun, and she and Brad talked while they worked, talked about their childhoods, talked about their difficulties in getting work in the areas they wanted. Brad went to interviews for illustrator jobs and came back dejected;

he was softly spoken, easily bruised. Looking out to the fig tree they talked of dreams and she asked him to illustrate her children's book, wanting his cartoons and his gentle humour in her book.

Gaylene and Brad spoke of their family and how they were faring in Darwin since William had enticed Glenda to join him there after six months on his own and she had packed up Scott and Katy and Salami the family sausage dog and left Bendigo to drive up through the Centre. Once she got there Glenda hated living in Darwin: she hated the heat, she missed her older children, and the place was too far away from everything and everyone she knew. Soon she would be back. Nobody seemed to know whether or not William would be coming back.

Gaylene loved living with Brad. She thinks now of his first day at kindergarten. She went with him as he would not go alone, had already been kept at home until he was four and a half. They wandered around and stood to watch a little boy drawing with crayons at a table; the boy dropped a crayon and Brad said he would get it but he took too long and she looked under the table to find him sitting there crying with the crayon in his hands and she crawled under the table and sat with him. He was vulnerable and she knew it and even though she was younger than him, tried to care for him, for his tender nature. As they grew up she was always the more confident, the more forthright, although he had more friends, fitted into places more easily than she did.

They have a kind of language; how she knows that language: a series of shared looks and messages mostly centred on their common love of animals. One day a friend of William's chased a sick-looking crow across a paddock and kicked it hard with one of his boots. Waiting in his car Gaylene and Brad did not say a word but they exchanged a look and from then on neither of them would speak to the friend but only shared that knowing look whenever they saw him.

Once Brad hid in the garden of the house in Wycheproof, hid until late: he had argued with Glenda, she was in a bad mood. Brad's dog, a pug named Candy, the dog given to him the Christmas before his sister was born, had played up: she was old, she smelled, she wheezed, she coughed, and that night Glenda had lashed out and said she was going to knock Candy on the head. And Brad had taken off into the garden to hide behind the inground tank with its clean cool smell, the tank they leant their legs against on a hot day when it was full, the one that gave out mosquito larvae or wrigglers, as they call them, in the water from the tap. When Glenda went out to call him, telling him what the rest of them were having for tea, what he was missing out on, he retreated further back into the sprawling canopy of the lemon tree in the yard.

Later he snuck around to the window of Gaylene's room, calling her with a loud whisper through the open window. He asked her to bring him food: a sandwich, biscuits, orange cordial. They talked about Candy. Glenda would not put her down, they would not let her. They would hide Candy if necessary. Glenda pretended not to notice the snacks going from the kitchen to the bedroom and the whispered conversation at the window. Candy lived, at least for a few months, until a vet said she must be put down as her heart disease had made her quality of life poor. They took the next few days off school. Brad hid under his doona, crying, sweating. Candy was thirteen, he fourteen and a half.

After being close as toddlers and children they had grown apart as teenagers; she watched him sometimes, living his life in Wycheproof. Boys had it easier than girls in that place, and she saw how he went to parties and kept his head down while she was forever sticking hers out, how he stayed close to the sprinkler-watered lawn of their house, spending afternoons hitting fallen apricots with his tennis racquet, slamming them into the side of a brick chimney, while she was not content to stay. She had to climb the hill and stand up there and look around to see what there must be to see, what surely must have changed since the last time she looked out over the paddocks. But Gaylene knew their bond remained fast.

In the Brunswick house he and Nicola had the front bedroom, looking out onto Weston Street, and she and Jude were in a room further back along the passage. In the mornings she listened for his bare feet as he walked up the passage to start his day's work at the desk under the window. She woke to the sound of Bucket's toenails clacking on the lino. She waited for a moment and then got dressed and walked through the house to join them in the sunshine that always seemed to seep through that window.

Glenda came back from Darwin without William during the time when Gaylene and Brad lived in Brunswick. With Scott having already made his coach and train trip to Melbourne, Glenda drove down through the desert, over the heat, over the days, with Katy in the passenger seat and Salami the sausage dog crouching under wet towels in the back. They went to Leo and Violet's house, and Scott met them there. They needed to stay with relatives until they could work out where they would live. News had travelled ahead of them by the time they got there. William had phoned. He was on his way down.

A few days later, perhaps a week, William arrived. He joined Glenda and Katy and then with his brother Jack he drove to Melbourne to visit his older children one afternoon. Gaylene had not seen him for a year.

He walked into the house. His beard was neatly trimmed, his hair was cut. From the back of the house she heard his hello through the open front door and she walked quickly along the lino-clad passage: she smiled at him all the way along that passage. Meeting him at the door she put her hands on his shoulders and kissed him; he looked surprised; she even kissed her uncle. She invited them inside and made them tea. As her father sipped from the cup she had made him she watched and thought of the card she had sent him months ago, and she hoped that he remembered: *Read between the lions*. She was too shy to tell him how much she missed him but wondered if it showed.

She asked about his leaving Darwin.

'After they drove away,' he said, 'I felt like I was seeing ghosts. I could hear the kids, see Glenda out by the pool, sitting on the steps. I rang work and made up a story about having to leave – family emergency – and gave the agents I'd rented the house from the same story, then packed up the Land Rover and took off. It was over.'

She loved him for those words. She understood.

But her parents and the twins had no house after this, seeming to be always on the move, migrating, never settling, shuffling from one place, one temporary home, to another. It was William's doing. Glenda wanted to settle and make a home, her feet on her own dirt, as badly as William seemed unable to settle and be still. William and Glenda decided to stay on in Melbourne for a while, close to their older children. Gaylene saw them hugging one another more often, heard softness in their voices when they spoke to one another. She wondered what it was. William's drive down, following his wife? Gaylene imagined a filmic view from above of their movements, their tracks over red dirt roads, linking them back together, husband and wife. Or could it have been the sight of their two older children reunited, having made a household together with rooms beside one another and with the sunny place at the back where they kept their hopes for future careers in books and folios that lay side by side? Or was it a much older bond that Gaylene did not know as well as she thought she did:

a bond dating from the romance on the road to the slaughterhouse?

Her parents rented the house in Elm Street. William took a job as a foreman at a meatworks in South Melbourne and Glenda started to work part-time at a shop in the city while Scott and Katy commenced their final years at high school. All of them knew without needing to speak the words that Elm Street was another temporary home, that the Melbourne lives of William and Glenda represented a momentary stasis, a time to rest before they packed up again: Elm Street did not feel like home. But next time, with another move, all would change. The situation would be different.

Plans for a house at Bushy's were underway. In his aluminium shed at Elm Street William was building a dream, a dream of a house, a family home. He drew up the plans; it was to be a mudbrick house of the local soil, the golden soil of Bushy's. William filled the shed with the pieces of the house in his dreams. He began sifting through markets and secondhand shops on the weekends. He collected fragments. He gathered old glass, flawed with the illusion of water in every pane, memories of sand, sea, river. He bought heavy lengths of timber from house wreckings and timber recyclers.

In the shed the home began to take shape and William and Jude formed a friendship. Jude too loves to dream of designing and building houses. When they visited her family Jude would disappear into the shed as soon as they passed through the gates. He walked up the driveway to seek out William. Jude and William spread out the house plans and drawings across the top of William's workbench and together they inspected the latest finds: lengths of redgum from an old house, leadlight glass, a pile of bluestones. And she would walk in, looking for Jude, and stay a while, absorbing the plans, seeing and hearing the house in her mind, believing in it, wanting to walk its floors, to see William and Glenda in their own house at Bushy's, the house and land alive with traces of memories.

At Bushy's too the house began to grow. When he could William spent weekends there, making prototypes of mudbricks, setting them to dry in the sun.

One day she saw them, saw the bricks lined up in rows, and she found they had a strange familiarity, bringing to mind an image of low gravestones, like a burial ground for soldiers who have been lost in a war in a distant country. The dirt was local but the bricks set up like that seemed exotic and dislocated, portentous.

As a little girl she went to Bushy's to visit her great-grandmother and great-uncle, the sister and brother who lived there. Many items at Bushy's interested her: the shadow box with its compartments filled with china dogs and silver horses and depression glass vases, the bottled fruit in screened cupboards on the side verandahs, the dead cars in the back paddock, the eggs in the chicken coops, the green bunyip money boxes slowly filling with copper coins that would be given to Gaylene and Brad at Christmas time. But nothing interested her as much as the music box that lived on a sideboard by the heavy dining table and chairs. Three china girls stood in a ring, hands linked, looking outwards, frozen in a garden dance in fancy dresses. They stood on a green base that could be turned to start the music, to start the spinning of the dancing girls. Every visit to Bushy's would see her going to the sideboard and making those girls spin to their hurdy-gurdy music.

When Gaylene was ten her great-grandmother Millicent gave the girls to her: Nan's girls, Glenda called them, and somehow she made her voice sound like Millicent's in that way she had, that way of putting the past into the now. Gaylene carried her precious gift home in her hands. Only a year later there would be no more visits to the house as Millicent's brother died and the contents of the house were auctioned. Millicent went to live with her son Digger, and then following his death she lived in a hospice, having grown frail, before dying in her hundredth year. All Gaylene had from Bushy's were the girls and throughout her life she carried them from house to house, most often in her hands as they were fragile and she did not trust wrapping and packing them with other less precious ornaments. She liked to know exactly where they were. Over the years she moved many times and every time the girls came with her, the girls were in her hands as she travelled between houses.

The girls were almost lost several times. Once the boyfriend with the Torana held the girls in one clumsy hand above Gaylene's head. She watched him consider smashing the girls on the floor beside her, beside her head, as once again he sat astride her chest, pinning down her arms. No doubt he saw the look on her face for he set down the girls and got up and left the room. She sat up, turned the green base, watched them dance one or two wobbly rotations, and then she hid them where he would not find them again. Soon she and the girls would be on the move.

The girls now live on her bookshelves at home in North Balwyn and often she holds them close, turns the base to hear the hurdy-gurdy and watch them dance, and to think of the place where they came from, the place where the family home is being built close to the old house that the ancestors built.

By the time William and Glenda and the twins were settled in Elm Street, Gaylene and Jude had moved to the clinker brick house in Maud Street, North Balwyn. Her parents came to live in her city, her place of seas and lighthouses, her place of silver skyscraper-lighthouses, and she soon roamed across the city as though moving suburbs was like moving streets in a country town. She did not consider that it might make a difference, that she was distancing herself from her family again, putting herself out of range, leaving Brad in Brunswick, the rest of them in Northcote.

But William kept travelling the distance to wander into their house with his gifts, not allowing Gaylene and Jude to be too far away. One day he turned up in a bright yellow ute that he had bought. She looked out of her corner window and laughed out loud to see how he had piled up the ute: strapped to the roof was the top of a dining table, its sculpted base standing in the back; the table was stained a deep red-brown and later she saw that it had softly bevelled edges and rounded corners. Jude went out to help William unload the pieces and William put the table together in the dining room. 'I made it for you,' he said to Gaylene. 'Been working on it in the shed for weeks. Had to throw a tarp over it every time this bloke came in to see me.' He nodded at Jude.

Next time William visited, an old desk was in the back of the ute. She had left her part-time job at the radio station and had enrolled in a university degree but she had nowhere to sit and work on her assignments and he knew it: 'I saw it at a market. Thought you'd like it. You could sand it off, do it up, or just leave it as it is. Bet you'll leave it.' She ran her hands over the musty timber, over the gentle warping of the top. He was right, for she did leave the desk unfinished and unrefined, liking the store of history that it seemed to have brought with itself, liking how it almost matched the splintering frames of the corner window of the bedroom, and she had her father and Jude put the desk in there, pushed under that corner window. She would sit at the old desk and look out over her assignments at her two views of the corner of her street.

Brad too returned to study. She heard from Glenda that he was studying town planning, wanting a career, wanting to leave the job at the video shop and use his skills in art and design. She saw him on Sunday nights at Elm Street, nearly always sat next to him at the table, but she heard about his break-up with Nicola only from Glenda and did not comment when she noticed his downcast expression at dinner.

Since her move across the city she and Brad seemed not as close.

Recently, though, after she visited him in hospital, sitting on the edge of his bed, seeing the needle bruises on his hands and hearing the wheeze in his throat, and after Bucket's disappearance ('*She drowned*'), the fine sibling webbing between them made itself felt again. And all of that was only short weeks ago. Days ago.

Now he lies in the channel and the night at Mama and Papa's house is darkening, quietening, slowing. His sister wants to stop the night from finishing, to keep it speeding onwards, keep it alive and teeming with memory and resonance and evidence of the lives of William and Brad, the lives of her family. She cannot think of sleeping.

9

Sunday, 3 January 1993, 3 am

Glenda tells Gaylene that a bed in one of the back bedrooms has been made up for her and Jude. But while others are falling asleep, flagging with exhaustion, Gaylene's blood feels hot and fast and thick.

Katy and her friends are asleep in the rumpus room: the lights are off, the sliding door is closed. And although Glenda says she will not sleep, she wants to lie down for a while. Her best friend takes her into the other back bedroom.

Gaylene and Jude sit at the table, left alone, quiet for a minute, pressed close together. With most of the lights in the house turned off it feels more like the house that she has known, the house that she has visited many times before tonight. Outside the noise of the storm settled hours ago but in the distance out over the lake sheet lightning still gives a weak flash and glow now and then, lighting up the strip of water that can be seen above the distant trees. Closer, between the house and the road, there are paddocks of mainly flat land with the softest of undulations. This is another landscape that she counts as hers, she knows those undulations: she can close her eyes and still see them flowing like the rise and fall of low surf. Near the house is a lawn that Leo and Violet keep watered, keep green, even now in mid-summer when the surrounding palette is yellow and gold and white and brown on the ground with the charcoal-dark trunks and grey-green leaves of ironbark above.

The door to the rumpus room rumbles gently along its rails and Scott emerges. He slides into a chair beside his sister. 'I was glad it was you who told me, you and Jude,' he says. 'Family. I would hate to have been told by the cops.'

Jude puts his arms on the tabletop, wrinkles the seersucker cloth, and lays his head on his arms.

Scott gets up. 'Jude should go to bed. So should you.'

'I won't sleep.'

'Me either. We should just lie down like Mum's doing.'

He is right. She stands up too and touches Jude's elbow; he is already starting to doze. Scott moves closer to her.

'I haven't hugged you yet,' he tells her, and he puts his arms around her. 'I love you,' he says. And she says it back. It is the first time they have ever thought to say it to one another.

In the bedroom Jude lies down on the bed. She climbs in but remains sitting up, her back against a wall; the light switch is within her reach but she cannot put off the light. She is too afraid of the dark, her fear almost as old as herself but different tonight, different now. Jude pulls the bed covers up to shade the direct light from his eyes and puts one arm across her legs.

'I'm here,' he says. 'Wake me if you need me.'

As a child her nightmares meant she could not bear to sleep in a dark room, wake in a dark room. And the fear followed her, dogged her into adolescence when the dreams grew more violent: she dreamt of murders, massacres, ragged bodies, murderers chasing victims, victims running and hiding. As she woke a noise would begin, a chaotic noise like all the keys of a piano being pressed at once, louder, louder, louder. She slept with her bedroom light on until she was twenty. Now she can sleep in a dark room but she hates to see the bare glass of a window at night, afraid of what or who might be looking in.

Jude's breathing smooths out. Listening to him is like listening to a heartbeat that she is afraid will skip. She cannot stand it. She slips out of the bed: perhaps Scott will still be up, maybe she will talk to him.

She steps into the passage that links the back bedrooms, a laundry and bathroom in between. Murmurs and quiet sobs come from behind the closed door of the other bedroom, from Glenda and her friend. Gaylene makes her footfalls quiet. This walk over the carpet through the uneasily resting house feels dangerous, booby-trapped: she could be crossing an unfamiliar world instead of a floor of Berber carpet.

The door to the kitchen and the rest of the house is closed. She slides it open and is about to step through the gap. Only one light in the kitchen is on: the orange bench glows and the area where the table and chairs are is dim; she is standing in the dark, she in her clothes that she pulled on in Maud Street, clothes that feel like they belong to a different person now.

Leo and Violet, Mama and Papa, are on the other side of the kitchen bench, the lit-up side. Mama is leaning back against the bench and Papa is embracing her. Both of them are crying. She has never seen either of them cry and she has never seen more heart-rending weeping. Even Glenda's weeping was less disturbing than this, perhaps because she did not hold it in; like Gaylene, Glenda let out her tears. But Leo and Violet have looked after their family all night, loved their family, opened their home to their family. Now, after three am, almost four, they are still up. With everyone else in the house gone to lie down, perhaps to sleep, Mama and Papa are still playing the leaders, like parents staying up later than everyone else, checking to see that all sleep safely, sleep soundly. Mama and Papa are standing in the centre of the house with their family sleeping in each of the rooms, radiating outwards from this couple. Now they cry. Now they weep for the loss of their eldest son and their eldest grandson, and perhaps for the loss of their family as it has been and as it will never be again.

Gaylene steps back, almost leaps back, before they can see her. But from the dark behind the doorway in the bedroom passage she watches them for a minute, hating herself a little for doing so, feeling like a child spying on adults but having no excuse at the age of twenty-three. She is weeping again, wanting to understand exactly what Mama and Papa's shock, pain, loss mean to them. They are proud parents, proud grandparents. She has seen the way they shine when William is around them. Gaylene knows how it feels to have that shine in herself: her father is funny, cheeky, irreverent; he makes people laugh, he makes people's faces soft, makes Mama and Papa's faces soft.

One at a time she looks at these people whom she deeply loves.

Mama. Violet. They share the name. Violet is Gaylene's middle name and she loves it, has always loved having her grandmother's name in her own like holding her hands, encircling her. Mama has never been like other grandmothers Gaylene has known. Her hair is fine, shiny, dyed the deep brown-black that it had been when she was young, set into loose curls yet always appearing natural. Many times as a child Gaylene watched Mama and her friends set one another's hair, winding strands onto plastic rollers each with a length of elastic and a bead at one end to secure the rolled hair; applying thick pink setting lotion; and then drying the hair with an old-fashioned hair dryer, the expanding pipe coiled inside a white leather beauty case. Somewhere there is a photograph of Violet in a Hawaiian print bikini, her dark hair curling to her waist.

When Gaylene thinks of Mama, and she often does, she thinks of moonstones, platinum, forget-me-nots, pink hydrangeas.

A few years ago Mama had breast cancer and lost a breast. Gaylene and Brad talked about it in the sunshine of the Brunswick house, spoke of how the saddest things seemed to happen to the nicest people. (*It hurts her, hurts her now, to hear Brad's voice in her head, saying such a thing. Nicest people. Saddest things.*) At the time she remembered Mama's garden in town, opposite the butchery, and how she had made a cubbyhouse between three pink hydrangea bushes with forget-me-nots at her feet and the scent of jasmine wafting from the vines on the fence. With that image in mind she thought of her grandmother's breasts as soft pink hydrangea flowers, and she told this to Brad: together they mourned Mama's loss.

Mama has some old jewellery, including a moonstone brooch, but Gaylene thinks of her with a strand of moonstones, a necklace, each flat, smoothly polished crystal framed by a delicate platinum circle. She has imagined this gift for Mama, perhaps out of the moonstone brooch and the platinum ring that Mama wears on her wedding finger, but perhaps too it is the strange opaque glow of the Wedgwood blue eyes. Each memory she has of Mama she counts as a gleaming moonstone and now she has one to add –

Mama crying – Mama grieving, seen in a new crystal of moonstone.

And Papa. He has a shiny pink bald head except for the grey hair around the ears and the back of the head. All his brothers look the same: bald head, pot belly. A couple of times, years ago, she went to parties in houses with warrens of pastel-painted rooms where the pink-domed brothers milled about with their wives and children and grandchildren. She loves him for his gentleness and for the way he pinches his grandchildren's cheeks and the way he loves the kangaroos that come to feed on his lawn early in the mornings and at dusk, and the way he says *sorry, mate* when he has to take a shovel and kill a brown snake that has come too close to the house. William has been joking for years about how Papa finds reasons to put off shooting the rabbits on his farmland for as long as he can, for he is fond of the rabbits, fond of all animals, just like his son, like William, and like all of William's children.

She has never been one to feel that she belongs anywhere but in Ironbark she does belong, if only a little. Her family has a history in this town, is part of its weave. Mama and Papa built up the butchery in the main street and made it into a family landmark and perhaps even a community landmark.

Gaylene is proud of that butchery, fiercely proud of its history, and now, looking at how her grandfather tilts his head towards his wife, she can see the tilt of a butcher's head as he focuses on the work on the block in front of him. Brad sketched William in that pose once, captured the likeness of the tilt of the butcher's head to the tilt of a man's head when he holds a lover who leans her head on his chest just as Mama now leans her head on Papa's chest.

She puts one hand lightly on the doorjamb and lowers her gaze from her grandparents, and she finds herself thinking of the strange ways the butchery business has helped to keep her father and herself, butcher and vegetarian, near to one another.

She has never walked through a functioning slaughterhouse and seen the blood sluice or heard the shrieks of animals on the killing floors, yet behind her she has the trails of two generations of butchers.

People often laugh at this genealogy of hers and say it is no wonder that she does not eat meat.

It was never that simple.

The old slaughterhouse owned by her family stands in a paddock amongst ironbark and wattle. That is where her father slit the throats of lambs when he was in his teens but now the slaughterhouse is dead, crumbling and splintering into the dirt. Not long before tonight she went to the slaughterhouse for a barbecue, standing back while her uncles the butchers set up the barbecue in the paddock and greased the hotplate with dripping.

A pile of old bullock skulls lay inside the gate: long yellow grasses had become entwined through the eye sockets, binding the skulls to the ground. The effect was of a shrub with horns for branches and empty eyes for flowers. As the meat seared on the barbecue she found herself glancing over her shoulders, imagining resonances of slit-throated lambs and headless bullocks. She ate the vegetable pie that Violet had brought for her and soon William drove up in his ute, come from the city; he flashed his headlights and they shone over Gaylene.

At eighteen, when she first lived away from home, she was at the tail end of a stage when many girls avoid their fathers or may even hate them. One day William sent around a gift wrapped in white butcher's paper and tied with the silky twine he used for threading together a rolled roast of beef. Inside was a chicken stuffed with turkey seasoning; it had been cooked until the skinless flesh gleamed pure white. He had spent hours boning the chicken and making the spicy stuffing: she could imagine his hands working the flesh for her. Even now she remembers William's skill with reluctant admiration, recalls his handling of knives, his delicacy as he trimmed and sliced, undertaking the brutal with precision and grace.

'A good butcher cuts himself only with a blunt knife,' he would say, flashing a knife around a steel, making lightning.

He gave her a parcel of meat every weekend back when she lived in Bendigo and was at her most distant from her family. He could have wrapped up cheap items – chops, hamburgers, mince – but instead she would find an array of fillet steaks that fitted into the palm of her hand, shish kebabs threaded with coloured vegetables and marinated meat, and samples from his twenty varieties of sausages. William and Gaylene did not speak much back then; wordlessly his gifts linked them together. But later when she became a vegetarian she could not help thinking that those meats in disguises had fooled her into not noticing that they were the flesh of animals her father had taught her to love.

William was an animal-loving butcher. He had ways of making animals, even wild animals, trust him. She would always remember watching him from the kitchen window in the house in the Mallee as he talked to a possum raiding the apricot tree. He stood in the dark for an hour until the possum came to him, ambling down the tree and crossing the verandah, letting itself be picked up and carried as placidly as an indoor cat. Inside the possum peered around the lounge room as the kids stroked its fur until William put it back in the apricot tree.

The same townspeople who bought meat from William knew of his compassion for animals. They brought orphaned joeys for his family to nurse; once they were given a baby emu and Gaylene nursed it in her lap, running her fingertips over the swirling pattern in the black and white fluff of its feathers.

In the pink-tiled butchery that was Leo's when Gaylene was a child, her uncles strung the S-shaped butcher's hooks into chains and they clanged together like outsized jewellery. But the butchers kept the hooks out of reach of the kids; the barbed ends could rip a finger in two. After all, they were designed for slipping into flesh.

At a fancy dress party for toddlers they dressed Gaylene as a fairy and Brad as a butcher. He wore one of William's striped aprons cut down to size and a clunking knife holder containing a plastic sword was strapped to his side. But he grew up to be an artist not a butcher. Once William came home from a duck-shooting outing; the one duck he had managed to shoot was drooping, dripping, from his finely shaped hands. Brad said that if William ever shot another duck he would never speak to him again. Gaylene sat in her chair in the lounge room that day and she watched Brad stand up to William: which side should she take? She loved them both, father and brother, but when she looked at that duck, its curved neck slipping between two of William's fingers, she knew that this time she was with Brad. She did not want to see any more ducks dead in her father's hands. Gaylene and Brad were children then, but people, adults, believed Brad when he spoke like he did that day. The duck went uneaten, thinly disguised in a layer of paper at the back of the fridge. William never shot another duck.

Gaylene cannot picture those hands, William's hands, with their long fingers and purple rivers of veins, smeared with blood. Yet countless times she visited him in his various butcheries. She stood by the block while he chopped and sliced and tenderised and she watched the bandsaw spraying him with bone fragments as he guided it through a side of beef.

It was not that long before tonight that she told her family she had become a vegetarian. Brad said in a quiet aside: 'I wish I could do that.' It was a Sunday dinner and the family was eating roast lamb. William was chewing on the shank. He said nothing, but Gaylene saw him lapsing into thought as he sucked out the marrow, smiling to himself.

He had taught her well with his lessons about respecting animals. She could not bring herself to harm an animal but she also could not choose between dog and calf, cat and lamb, lyrebird and chicken. Now, knowing what has taken place at the channel, knowing about the involvement of Max the dog, she starts to wonder if perhaps William taught his children to love animals too much. And she wonders if an animal-loving butcher is possibly the most dangerous kind of butcher.

Leo and Violet cry softly.

Gaylene had seen her father cry only a handful of times. The first was the day he saw a man crushed to death at a meatworks while he and others screamed out warnings that went unheard over noisy machinery. The second was at a rubbish tip one afternoon in the Mallee. He held a seagull with a slug piercing its neck. A car full of teenagers – *gutless*, he shouted after them – sped away with the barrel of a gun poking from a back window. He made his kids wait in his car while he smashed the head of the squawking seagull with a rock. When he returned to the car Gaylene saw him push away tears with the back of his hand before he revved up the chuggy motor and drove home.

Tonight she thinks a dark sky's worth of fabric will not be enough for how much his parents need to cry: for how much every person breathing, shuffling, sweating, turning and stirring in this hushed house needs to cry.

10

Sunday, 3 January 1993, 4 am

Gaylene moves away from the sliding door and goes back into the bedroom.

Jude is sound asleep.

The night is both filling and emptying, she thinks she can feel it like a drawing in and out of tides. The night is filling with stories, memories, hauntings, but as dawn approaches, the night empties of hope and a cocoon threads itself around the lives of her father and her brother as though by morning the very last opening of the cocoon will close.

Her grandfather Digger died a couple of years ago and Gaylene sat on a pew at the funeral and listened to Millicent, Digger's mother, mourning. Millicent was almost one hundred and her only child had just died of age-related causes: she had outlived him. And Gaylene had absorbed the grief and the bitterness of Millicent's longevity, of being the one left behind, last, to bury her loved ones.

Here in this room Gaylene feels a grave-dark dread rising in her: the dread of being a survivor. She cannot comprehend what William and Brad themselves have lost (their lives: *their lives*); it is more than enough to know what the world has lost and what she herself has lost.

The blind on the window is closed but it does not quite fit the pane; Gaylene spies the thinnest edge of black around the blind's pale rectangle. She slips into the bed, trembling, crying silently to see the black edge, black wedge.

Every scary thought and image from the worst of her lifetime's bad dreams and her fear of the dark are here crowding in at the outline of black glass. She sees the legions of murderers and mutilated bodies that have chased her through dreams all the way from childhood. From the earliest dream that she remembers, a fat butcher from the Donald meatworks strides to the window. He is dressed in a blood-soaked white butcher's coat and gumboots and he whips out a knife from his keeper to glint in the night. Once she saw a boy die. She was six and he was four. He had an illness and one day he was standing on his porch teasing and taunting her as she waited for a school bus in front of his house, and he slumped over the porch railings and his voice broke off and his eyes bulged out of his head. She felt a buzzing feeling in her mind and then she heard the noise, a sound like all the keys on a piano being pressed at once. And now his bulging eyes are looking through the glass at the window's edge. The baby is there, the pink baby, the glowing baby that was hers and has never left her mind, never left her memories. A pink baby's face flickers like a weak candle flame at the glass. Her ghosts, her dream ghosts, her night ghosts, etch themselves into her vision, and here is William, here is her dad, pulled from the water, a body, a corpse, and Brad, her brother, floats past in the distance, underwater, limp, lifeless, alone.

The dead are at the window. The dead are close, too close, at the edges of her skin now, yet she feels that she has no skin; she is falling to pieces, dispersing, disintegrating, a flood, a gush, a body of water. She feels herself collapsing as though William and Brad were part of her body's framework; they loved her to the bones, they were the bones of her, part of what held her up. Earlier she had told herself that families work out matters of love, that love neatly balances itself into equal portions. Now she thinks this is a lie. Love is not equal. Love is not fair. She silently screams to herself, to the window, to the dead. The people she loves the most, *loves the most*, at this point in time are Dad and Brad, the two that are gone, the two that are dead. She feels that at least two-thirds of herself are as dead as the dead gathered at the window. She cannot imagine seeing in the morning, getting up out of this bed and walking out to breathe the air and feel the sun or the rain on her face when William and Brad will not walk again except in the dreams and the memories of those left in this house.

And Brad is in the water, shifting with the currents. Perhaps he will be taken all the way to the Mallee. He may never come to the surface, she might never know where he lies, Brad left forever under the water somewhere between the lake and the Mallee wheatfields, the channel like an artery pumping between the landscapes and waterscapes of all of the family's lives, disappearing and decomposing into water, into memory, into a well of grief. The bad dream noise pounds in her head.

Gaylene lies down beside Jude and closes her eyes to rest them from the gleaming black chink of window. She does not sleep. Before her closed eyes a story with uneven lapping edges begins. All of a sudden she seems to have known this story forever.

11

The channel

The Bushy's dirt around William's feet is light clay and its colour is almost gold this morning. William has a green hose in his hands and brown water spurts hotly from one end of it. He knows the value of water but he knows too that dogs get thirsty on a hot day. Max, the black Labrador, leaps into the air to gulp the water, higher, higher, and Glenda snaps a picture.

In a while Brad's car pulls up beside the hired caravan. Brad and Katy and Marcus have driven up from Melbourne for the day, and the lot of them sit out at the block drinking a few cold beers from an esky full of clinking melting ice from the service station in town. They sit by the foundations of the house, the dirt compacted and bare amidst the yellow grass. On the other side of these foundations the old house stands, the house of timber and mud that Sarah and Dugald, the ancestors from Scotland, built in the late eighteen fifties. Nobody has lived in it since 1979 and since then its walls have warped and vandals have shot rifle holes in the mud sections and have pillaged its bits and pieces such as the remains of the iron woodstove in the outdoor kitchen with its hard swept earthen floor, but the house still stands, still lives.

The day grows hotter. It is time for a swim. Every day William has been swimming in the channel, the irrigation channel that is a couple of minutes drive away, the channel that most of the town swims in on a hot day, the channel where he has been swimming since he was a kid. The lake feeds the channel and then it runs northeast, goes all the way through the Mallee, irrigating wheat, watering sheep. Tourists camp out at the lake caravan park or at the camping ground on the other side, people who want to waterski, families with young children. Many of the locals avoid the baked warm stinky mud of the lake, the shallow lukewarm water that takes an age to wade through before a swimmer is in over his head. But the channel is deep and cool with sharply sloping banks that a swimmer scuttles down before plunging in. He is up to his neck in a second: the currents grab him and he drifts downstream and the pull is fast, smooth, driven, and he goes with it for a minute before stroking inwards to the bank, cutting across the pull of the currents and then floating out to do it again.

Then there are the bridges with churning white water around the legs, where the teenage boys, the hoons of the town, go for the best thrills. They bomb and duck and make out they are in a raging river, spreading themselves on their backs, their limbs sticking out, sunburned, peeling. They go with the flow, splattering and tumbling to reach the edge and then ambling out over the bank to run back to the bridge and do it all again.

And there is the dropbar, the place where the flow is regulated with a drop of a metre in the water level. A swimmer can go over the top of it, like cresting a waterfall: the locals do it all the time, have been doing it for years.

William, Brad, Katy and Marcus pile into William's ute. They try to coax Glenda to come with them but she will not, she shakes her head at the idea of herself swimming in the channel, the bloody channel, although surely she swam there as a girl, and she waves them off. With a fat romance novel open on her lap she sits in a deckchair in the shade.

Max heaves himself into the back of the ute as it moves off down the track.

They stop at the channel and take a deep cool dip and then sit around in the ute, parked in the shade, the doors flung open. Brad pushes a tape into the deck and a song comes on, it is the Red Hot Chili Peppers and the song is 'Under the Bridge'. He tells Katy that he loves this song and the four of them listen, looking out at the dry summer grass, ironbark trees looming from across the road. William talks of his love of the bush and says he wants to be buried out in the bush when he falls off the perch. Katy and Brad laugh at him, laugh to remember how for years their dad has said that when he dies he wants the family to stuff him in a seated position, stick him in a comfortable armchair, and use him as a hat stand. And then Brad with his soft young voice speaks out over the music and says he too would want to be buried in the bush, not stuck under marble in a cemetery.

Anyway, he says, and he smiles at them all, head flung back, hair wet, chest bare and pale: I am going to live forever.

They are hot again. William says Glenda will be getting worried as they said they were going for just a quick swim and here they have sat around and it is time they headed back. But there is talk of one more dip, a last cool-down, straight in, straight out, at the dropbar: that is always good value, good fun, a bit of current, a bit of churn.

The ute pulls up on a slant at the edge of the bank. They get out. Doors slam. William reminds them to hurry up, make it quick. A couple of fishermen are way down on the nearest bridge, lines in the water, but otherwise they have the place to themselves. By the ute Katy slips out of the summer pants she has on over her bikini bottom while Marcus is getting ready a little way down the bank. William and Brad are closer to the edge.

Katy glances at the channel and sees Max the dog out in the water, already over on the far side, below the dropbar, in the swirling currents. And that water looks wild today. The dog is struggling, he bobs up and down frantically, frantically enough to worry Katy. She shouts and as she does she sees Brad, sees her brother run down the bank and dive into the water, fast and silent, close to where the brown water falls over the dropbar.

Her father comes hurtling over the top of the dropbar – she has not even seen him enter the water – and quickly her father and her brother, William and Brad, go under.

And she laughs. She thinks they are clowning, being tossed about a little by the water, as though at any minute William's skinny legs will stick up as he does a handstand. It has been a happy day and she laughs.

Marcus is at her side. They're in trouble, he shouts.

She moves before she takes in the words.

Katy runs to William's ute, looking in the back, grabbing a tangle of rope, and then Marcus has the other end. They are furiously untangling the snarls. And Marcus runs to the water's edge with his end of the rope and she runs after him, and Marcus throws the rope across the water. The currents toss the rope away, skew it, loop it, deflect it.

Katy sees William and Brad go under three times. Once they emerge and she notices that their eyes are open but they seem to be unseeing – blind, dream-faced – and neither man reacts to Katy and Marcus's shouts from the edge. They make no sound other than one diminishing call from William that Marcus hears: a call of help before he goes under again. Both men disappear, the brown water sealed and opaque. They emerge again, unseeing, unhearing, unmoving except for the way the water moves them: thrusting and lifting and collapsing them like they are buoys. The rope does not get anywhere near them: it is a writhing bouncing eel in the chop and churn of the currents.

Lacing the rope around one of his wrists Marcus goes in. He tries and tries to swim to them but today the channel is not to be swum. It is not water for swimming, it is water for dying. William and Brad reappear through the surface again, and this time it is William's back instead of his face that emerges. Katy sees it. She shouts and points to the white gleaming hump in the brown. Katy sees Marcus almost reach her father's back, he could just about stretch out his fingers and touch William's skin. But the hump shrinks, then turns slightly and disappears, and Marcus is tossed away towards the bank.

Katy sees that the water has closed over William and Brad again. In her hands she holds the end of the rope. Marcus's life perhaps depends on her holding this rope but William and Brad are under the water and in her mind she cannot escape the image of their blind open eyes. She cannot help herself. She must do it, take the chance, take the risk, do it for Dad, for Brad. She coils the end of the rope around a tussock of grass at the top of the steep stony bank and leaves Marcus in the water, holding on to the other end of the rope. She runs along the edge, over the stones in her bare feet, screaming their names, looking to see if they have passed on from the ragged edge of the dropbar to the smooth sleek stream of brown stretching on toward the bridge. She runs back to the rope, picks it up, tries to haul Marcus in, but she is a tiny girl, light, thin, and he is tall, rangy, heavy-boned, and the water has hold of him, and she cannot find the strength to pull him out of there.

Katy screams, using all of her scant weight, her feet digging into the stones, the rope taut as a tightrope walker's line, screaming, screaming, knowing that she cannot keep holding on for a moment longer. At the bridge the two men fishing see her, hear her, run for their car and drive towards her. They take the rope and pull Marcus in and he collapses on the stones, his eyes closed, his chest heaving. And Katy runs along the bank, back and forth, back and forth: calling, calling their names.

By now a woman has come from a nearby house, a house with a windmill, her father a water board employee. She has called the police. She follows the thin girl. Katy tells her: Dad and Brad, my father, my brother. They're still in there. Still under the water.

They'll find them, the woman says, and she puts an arm around the girl. Katy is eighteen but she looks fourteen, especially today, especially now. Katy shrugs her off and she keeps running, calling the names. She passes Marcus and he opens his eyes and they are the darkest of shifting blues, dark sea blue, and he can barely talk with the water he has swallowed, and with the exhaustion, the defeat, the pain.

Are they gone? he asks, and it is the saddest voice she has ever heard.

I don't know, she answers, and she leaves him, goes to scan the banks again, to strain her eyes in the effort to see through the brown water, the mud-brown, blood-thick water, to see them, to reach them, to save them.

The police are here, and an ambulance. They take in the scene and nobody moves too quickly, not once they are told what has happened and how long ago it took place. Only Katy moves quickly, manic in her movements, telling them to get her father and her brother out of there. The police want to tell someone in the family, summon them here. They talk of reaching her mother or calling Leo and Violet but Katy shakes her head. She cannot think of that pain yet, of that finality. They can be found before then, they will resurface again, they will appear at the top of the water – a face, a limb, a back – and this time the police will be here and they will reach them, they will know how to get them out, and the ambulance is here: they will be resuscitated. They will cough and choke and splutter and open their eyes, yes, open their eyes and look around. They will speak and later tell the story of what happened to them once at the channel. Nobody will have to hear anything of it until they are safe and breathing and on dry land.

Katy looks across the surface, checking its every disturbance, but the jagged frill of the dropbar cuts through the flat sleek closed meniscus. There are colours, textures, breakages, tears, but only water.

The police still want to call someone. They want someone to look after Katy and Marcus. She thinks of Stretch, Marcus's father, William's brother, and lets the police call him. Stretch gets there fast and Katy is in front of him: she cannot stop screaming, cannot stop running around, breaking away, taking off down the banks again. But he grabs her. He wraps his strong butcher's arms around her shoulders and back and squeezes her hard to his chest to break her out of the frenzy. He looks into her face and tells her that it is time for them to leave the channel, leave the police to their work of finding William and Brad. They get Marcus into Stretch's car. Katy hesitates. Stretch is firm.

She looks out at the water one last time: one last time in this place at least, for the vision is not to leave her. The dream-eyes will not leave her. And on the other side of the channel she sees a flash of black that she has been looking over, looking past, in her search for Dad and Brad. Max the dog has paddled a long time, for hours have passed now since the ute pulled up here beside the dropbar. Hours have skimmed like seconds and the dog has not gone under. The dog is swimming. Katy runs to the policemen: the state emergency service workers have arrived and she points to the dog and begs them to bring him out of the water before he exhausts himself, before he can no longer swim. The men are reluctant but she begs. Please. Please don't let the water take him too. They use a winch and harness to drag in the dog, pulling him up from the water and onto the ground.

He struggles up on his belly over the stones; his legs are useless, his fur is heavy with water, and he lies with his legs sticking out on all sides, he pants and pants, the pink tongue limp on the yellow dirt. Stretch picks up the drenched dog and puts him in the back of his car and then he helps Katy into the front seat and straps a seatbelt around her.

Stretch gets in, starts to drive away. Katy turns for her last chance of glimpsing Dad and Brad. It will never feel right to leave them behind, so close, right there, somewhere.

And from now on a part of Gaylene is here at the channel with Katy, with Marcus, with all of her family, with her father and her brother. Sometimes she sees the brown water turn clear and she can see William and Brad under the water. She may look at them:

sleeping, dreaming, with closed-eyed faces, and they pass by her, near, so near. But she cannot touch them. They are out of her reach.

Gone under.

TEN YEARS LATER

The channel held on to Brad for three nights.

The time was long for my family and friends as we stayed on in Leo and Violet's house. We were in waiting, unable to begin to grieve while Brad drifted through the water and William lay in a morgue.

The channel was dangerous for the searchers. The water authorities would not turn down the flow as farmers needed the water for irrigation. A man who lived near the channel said he had not seen the channel run higher or faster in sixty years. The police said that even if William and Brad had been wearing life jackets they would have been unlikely to survive the water below the dropbar that day. They said that

Brad's body would resurface, that bodies sink to the bottom first and then after a time they float to the top. We waited. Hours and then days passed and Brad did not resurface. We were told that the police had strung a net from the bridge downstream. The thought hurt: a net, a bridge, and my brother's body to be caught and trussed up, fish-like.

I never went to the channel while the rescuers were there. I imagined a motley gathering of local men come to help, family members come to watch over, and police workers wanting to finish the job and write their reports and give the family a sense of closure.

Two days after the drownings I went with Jude, Katy, Scott and Marcus to the channel once the police had gone for the day. We parked near the bridge and walked along one bank to the dropbar. As my feet crunched on the stones and I looked ahead to the turbulent water I lost my last trace of hope that Brad could be found alive, perhaps disoriented, somewhere way down on the edge of the bank. I saw and felt the might of the water and I knew that my brother had not survived.

Katy had brought a posy to the water, a bunch of flowers that she planned to put into the water and let float away with the currents. But when she got there she told me that the water had already taken enough. She lay the posy in the grass by the edge, by the place where Brad had entered, the place she in her bare feet had run past again and again.

It was a quiet day with a light breeze that stirred the sails of the windmill. The noise of the water being chopped up over the dropbar broke the quietness. I crossed the bridge, pausing to look at the skeins of rope secured over the rails of the bridge; on the concrete side of the bridge the words 'Police Operation: Do Not Touch' had been chalked. I closed my eyes, picturing Brad, still seeing him sleeping, in chambray, in jeans.

Afterwards Glenda went to the channel with my father's sister, Rosemary. She said that before she left she moved close to the edge of the water and said, 'Come on, boy. You always say that you do what Mum tells you. Now come out of there.'

The next day, Tuesday, the police drove up Leo and Violet's driveway and two local policemen got out of the car, their caps removed. Brad was found. He had been caught in the net and drawn out of the water. We never saw his body. He was bloated and black, a funeral director said, best to remember him as he had been in life.

Bloated and black. When I heard that, I had to run from the room, run from the sound of the words.

Due to their untimely deaths my father and my brother underwent autopsies – *thrown to the lions*, Marcus said – before they were buried. Images of glittering instruments, bone saws, rib spreaders, knives: I could not keep them from my mind. My father could have seen the black humour of a butcher ending up sawn open and dissected on a table. But what of Brad? I could eke up no justice, poetic or otherwise, in his lying on such a table. Instead I mentally placed him at his drawing table under the window at the Brunswick house we shared. I sat him at the table and had him pencil the folded wings of an owl on his paper, a gift for Glenda. His dog Bucket's toenails clacked on the lino and his tabby cat purred and rubbed his head against the dog's muzzle.

Afterwards this tabby cat came to live with me.

On the Friday there was a funeral in the church where William and Glenda were married and where Brad and I were christened. None of us were church-goers but it seemed right to have the funeral service in that church in Ironbark, with its links to family history.

From all of the towns where my family had lived, people came to the funeral. The rain was gone, the day was hot, and the church overflowed. I wore the dark-blue floral dress that I had bought to wear to Toby and Jess's wedding on the day when my family had all been together.

Afterwards my mother, one of my uncles, Jude and I travelled down the main street, past the pink-tiled family butchery and on to the cemetery.

My uncle Jack and his wife Regina guided me to the gravesides after the interment. I scattered a handful of eucalyptus blossoms into the graves and as I did I looked down and saw my father's full name engraved on a silver plaque on top of his coffin. I was dizzy. Jack held on to my shoulders as my body wavered unsteadily. I could not bring myself to move away from the graves.

In the near distance I saw a vision of Bushy's in springtime, green and lush, the wildflowers blooming. My father and my brother Brad stood side by side in front of the pegged-out foundations of the house that Dad was to build. Both men were smiling directly at me. I watched them for a moment and then I told my uncle that I was ready to walk away.

I am sitting at the desk that my father gave me, its dark warped top still unsanded and unfinished, history intact. A pile of notebooks lies on the desk: notebooks filled with my handwritten memories of the day when the tragedy cut through my family like the swiftest of brown water channels.

The desk and I are now in an old white weatherboard house in the Dandenong Ranges; it is Jude's and mine, the first home that we have owned. We live here with our child, a boy, born in 2000.

The house is set high on a crest and has a sea of deep green grass flowing around its footings. Once

MIDNIGHT WATER

I imagined that the house my father was to build would have the sound of wind chimes, as Dad would hang chimes from the eaves. Tonight the weather is rainy but even on a clear day or night I think that the sound of our house is one of water, of rain on green, of our child's bare feet slapping on the cool clean pine floorboards with swirls of waves in the grain.

There is a blue couch in the middle of the lounge room and I like to lie on the couch and watch the rain come down in swathes. Near the blue couch is a low table that Jude crafted from ironbark. The table has a whorl of a knot near one corner and in the centre of the tabletop he has inlaid a rectangle of metal that is burnished to glisten with pools of blue and purple and copper.

The house unfolds itself into the garden, into the forest across the road, and into our plans. Although it is late Jude is walking about the house knocking on walls and running his fingers over picture rails and skirting boards. Together we dream about what we will make of the house. Fragments of what it will be gather in our minds: light, space, a bathroom in which I will place clusters of jade-green shattered glass tiles. My mother gave me the tiles. They were taken out during renovations of the house that Glenda lives in now: a solid brick house with pale rendered walls and a garden rich with fruit trees and roses, in the town of Ironbark.

Our child is tucked up in bed, sleeping through the sound of the pouring rain, as Jude comes to me and we put our arms around each other and look through the windows at the night sea of garden and talk warmly about the past.

Acknowledgements

With warmest love, I thank my husband and our child for their support. I wrote this book through late nights and early mornings as they slept and I am grateful to them for allowing me to do that, and for putting up with my slightly haunted self throughout the duration of writing.

I thank my family for being what they are: close-knit, loving and possessing of much good humour. I hope that my book may bring them joy and healing. Special thanks to my sister for telling me, that night, her story of what happened at the channel and for her very generous support for my writing the book.

Love to my friends who have shared the excitement of seeing the book to publication. Enjoy.

Thank you to Gerald Murnane, especially for the time he spent with me in his office at Grendon in the early weeks of 1993, helping me to piece together the first fragments of my writing about the tragedy.

To those who have gifted me with much encouragement for my writing over many years, thank you so very much, especially Andrea Goldsmith, Kevin Brophy and Judith Rodriguez.

Sincere thanks to Sari Smith whose words in a random conversation turned the writing of the book around and led it to its current form. Thanks also to Tess Brady for her interest as I worked on my early drafts.

Thank you to Jenny Darling for her unwavering enthusiasm and to Nikki Christer, Karen Penning and Jo Jarrah for helping me to bring the book to its final shape.

An earlier version of Chapter 9 was published in *Meanjin*, and their interest in my writing is much appreciated.

The lines from 'Five Bells' by Kenneth Slessor have been reproduced with the kind permission of Paul Slessor.

GAYLENE PERRY lives with her husband and child in the Dandenong Ranges near Melbourne, where she is currently writing a second book. She teaches in the Professional Writing department at Deakin University.